HORSE-DRAWN COMMERCIAL VEHICLES

255 Illustrations of Nineteenth-Century Stagecoaches, Delivery Wagons, Fire Engines, etc.

Edited by Don H. Berkebile

DOVER PUBLICATIONS, INC., New York

Copyright © 1989 by Dover Publications, Inc.
All rights reserved under Pan American and International Copyright Conventions.

Published in Canada by General Publishing Company, Ltd., 30 Lesmill Road, Don Mills, Toronto, Ontario.
Published in the United Kingdom by Constable and Company, Ltd., 10 Orange Street, London WC2H 7EG.

Horse-Drawn Commercial Vehicles: 255 Illustrations of Nineteenth-Century Stagecoaches, Delivery Wagons, Fire Engines, etc. is a new work, first published by Dover Publications, Inc., in 1989.

DOVER *Pictorial Archive* SERIES

Manufactured in the United States of America
Dover Publications, Inc., 31 East 2nd Street, Mineola, N.Y. 11501

Library of Congress Cataloging-in-Publication Data

Berkebile, Donald H.
    Horse-drawn commercial vehicles : 255 illustrations of nineteenth-century stagecoaches, delivery wagons, fire engines, etc. / edited by Don H. Berkebile.
        p.   cm.—(Dover pictorial archive series)
    ISBN 0-486-26020-8
    1. Wagons—United States.   I. Title.   II. Series.
TS2025.B47   1989
688.6—dc20   89-31365
                                                                          CIP

INTRODUCTION

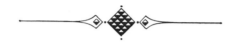

LONG BEFORE THERE WAS A NEED FOR personal vehicular transportation in colonial America, there was the necessity of moving goods and raw materials. Pack animals were sometimes used, but they could not carry all materials, nor were they efficient, so the first real demand on the wheelwright was for the construction of work vehicles. Two such artisans were sent from England to the Massachusetts Bay Colony in 1629. For over a century, the principal function of wheelwrights was to construct wheels for carts and wagons for the farm, for there was as yet little personal, industrial or commercial need for these vehicles. Exceptions could be found in such places as seaports, where cargoes had to be carried to and from ships, and in towns large enough to have substantial horse traffic, which necessitated the removal of manure from the streets. New York City, for example, had 20 licensed "car men" in 1676, their purpose being both to carry goods and remove manure.

Farm vehicles were often small and crude, sometimes with spoked wheels, but in other instances, with disk wheels that were either cut from logs or made from several flat pieces. Such vehicles could be readily constructed in any isolated area without the aid of a skilled mechanic, as reported by Johann David Schoepf, in *Travels in the Confederation, 1783–1784,* on his trip through southern Pennsylvania: "they use, however, little wagons for farming purposes furnished only with block-wheels, and these every farmer can make for himself without great trouble, by sawing disks out of fairly round timber-trees, and boring a hole in the middle for the axle." Even the refinement of this primitive wheel was not always required, for the sledge was a common means of moving things, sometimes even in the summer.

By the mid-eighteenth century several types of commercial vehicles were becoming prominent. The Conestoga wagon was used to carry freight and produce in Pennsylvania (later in Maryland); other areas had freight wagons but, lacking so distinctive a name, they are not as well known to us. For the movement of passengers, the stage wagon came into use. In its earliest form, it was nothing more than a covered wagon with benches inside. For freight movement within cities, there was the ubiquitous two-wheel dray. All of these vehicles retained their importance into the nineteenth century, the stage wagon evolving into the famous Troy and Concord coaches during the 1820s, the latter continuing to be manufactured and used into the early years of the twentieth century. The two-wheel dray was also used into the twentieth century, almost without change, because of the serviceability of its primitive design. Intracity freight movement was also facilitated by variations of the ordinary farm wagon and cart.

Little significant advancement occurred in the design of work vehicles during the early part of the nineteenth century, aside from the important changes in stages and the development, at about the same time, of the public omnibus. Several innovations in suspension, borrowed from the English and French, were soon applied to America's commercial carriers. Elliptic springs, platform springs and truck springs substantially altered both the design and the efficiency of all classes of vehicles, from the lightest to the heaviest, to serve the varying needs of the nation's commerce and industry. Inventive American mechanics began to patent many new features, not only of vehicle components, but also of machines and tools that produced the components with greater speed, ease and accuracy.

While this activity became increasingly evident from the 1830s and 1840s onward, the full effects of this gradual change were not seen until the final quarter of the century.

During the 1850s, the growth of the vehicle industry was reflected by the emergence of trade literature. In 1853, C. W. Saladee, of Columbus, Ohio, introduced his *Coach-makers' Guide,* succeeded in 1855 by *The Coach-makers' Illustrated Magazine.* In 1858 came Ezra Stratton's *New York Coach-makers' Magazine,* which in 1871 was absorbed into *The Hub,* soon to become one of America's two leading carriage journals. The other leader started in 1865 under the title *Coach-maker's International Journal,* acquiring the better-known title *The Carriage Monthly* in 1873. Although the titles of these publications suggest that they were devoted exclusively to the carriage business, they also gave extensive coverage to all sorts of commercial vehicles. In addition, beginning in the sixties, trade catalogs were issued by some builders, so that we have a complete and accurate record of the many types of working vehicles that were in use from that time onward. It is largely from this record that the illustrations in this volume have been chosen.

During the last quarter of the century, as the effects of the American industrial revolution finally overtook the trade, the carriage industry emerged from the handcraft stage. As the seventies began, machinery was only in limited use (mainly for sawing); carriage builders were of the general opinion that machinery could not be effectively employed in any but the largest factories. The first widespread use of mass-production techniques in the trade began in several Cincinnati carriage shops during the mid-seventies. Specialized machines processed the many wood parts of a carriage, and malleable iron castings minimized the labor of the smith shop by eliminating many hours of forge work. The castings, along with numerous other parts, were not made in the carriage shops, but were produced by the growing numbers of specialty-parts manufacturers. Thus, as gear and body irons, axles, wheels, springs, lamps, dashes, whip sockets, top fittings, shafts and other bentwood parts were purchased, the carriage builder became more of an assembler and finisher.

While this method of manufacture was initially developed for light-carriage construction, the relatively straight lines of the typical work vehicle were equally suited to mass production. The result of this increased ease and efficiency in wagon building was a less expensive vehicle, so that by 1900, economy versions of the more simplified delivery wagons could be purchased for less than $40, enabling even small businesses to own them. To keep up with the demands of an expanding market, manufacturers devised more sophisticated machinery. Improvements in drop forges, for example, resulted in some substitution of drop forgings for malleable iron castings, upgrading the quality of the work.

Even in the face of mass production, however, to the very end of the horse-drawn era, many wagons, particularly the lighter class, remained the product of small shops. As previously mentioned, all of the components could be purchased from specialty manufacturers. Eventually, even complete running gears and bodies could be purchased in-the-white (unpainted), put together in a small shop and painted, and the price could be competitive with that of the mass-produced wagon. Commercial vehicles usually had very little trimming, and even the cushion for the driver's seat could be purchased ready-made. Thus many vehicles came from a one-man shop, or shops where perhaps one or several sons worked with their father. In such cases it could almost be said that these were not manufacturers, but assemblers, painters and retailers. Likewise, many heavier wagons were also partially handmade, often to a greater extent than the light wagons, for the heavier wagons were sometimes custom work, specifically designed for a particular task. Such wagons were built both in small shops and in the factories of large firms, where custom work was turned out alongside the more standardized products of the assembly lines.

The heyday of the horse-drawn commercial vehicle was the last decades of the nineteenth century and the first decade of the twentieth. Colorful wagons of all types crowded the streets, especially in the larger cities. Many were artistically decorated, serving as billboards advertising the owner's business. Indeed, some were so decorative and impractical in design that they were more advertisements than carriers, in which instances they were often supplemented by the more serviceable wagons owned by the same firms.

The motortruck did not quickly supplant the horse-drawn wagon. During the early years of the motor age, too many manufacturers believed they could simply place a truck body on an automobile chassis. Not only was this practice a failure, but it also bred a suspicion of motortrucks in the minds of many early users who had been "stung" by a bad product. Later, even as motortrucks improved, these wary businessmen were slow to try a second venture. Also, many larger firms, having substantial investments in sizable fleets of serviceable wagons, trucks and drays, were understandably reluctant to scrap these slow but reliable carriers in favor of a comparatively expensive truck of unknown quality. One clever truck manufacturer tried to tempt this segment of the market by offering a truck-tractor in which the user simply eliminated the front axle and wheels of his horse-drawn vehicle and backed the tractor under the body to replace them and the horses, thus originating the semitrailer. By the mid-teens, many good motortrucks had become available and men, gradually losing their suspicions, began to replace the horse-drawn carriers.

Horses and motor vehicles shared the streets for a quarter of a century, however, for even in the twenties many wagons could still be found. Firms that made routine deliveries, such as dairies, bakeries and ice companies, continued to maintain horse-drawn fleets throughout the 1920s and into the 1930s. Incredibly, even in the mid-twenties, after the motor vehicle had made such a tremendous showing, there were those who believed that, while passengers might move by motor vehicle, the bulk of intracity freight would always move by horse, and some horse breeders were concerned with developing bigger and stronger horses to compete with trucks. By the advent of World War II, most wagons probably would have been left to rot, but a few held on because of wartime shortages. Even today, an occasional example can be found in use for hucksering and junk dealing.

The vehicles represented in this book have been arranged according to type in the following manner: carts (nos. 1–14); bandwagons (nos. 15 & 16); special-purpose heavy wagons (nos. 17 & 18); brewers' and bottlers' wagons (nos. 19–24); hearses (nos. 25–36); ambulances (nos. 37–44); camping wagons (nos. 45–47); peddlers' wagons (nos. 48–51); lunch and food wagons (nos. 52–57); farm wagons (nos. 58–69); sleds (nos. 70–79); coal and ice wagons (nos. 80–87); trucks (nos. 88–100); drays (nos. 101–105); express wagons (nos. 106–114); public vehicles (nos. 115–152); fire and police vehicles (nos. 153–164); tank wagons and sweepers (nos. 165–170); road-building, track-laying and miscellaneous vehicles (171–175); Conestoga wagons (nos. 176 & 177); delivery wagons (nos. 178–223); milk wagons (nos. 224–228); open delivery wagons (nos. 229–233); heavy delivery wagons (nos. 234–237); dump wagons (nos. 238–241). Information on striping designs is presented in nos. 242–244; nos. 245–255 show various harnesses.

Since this collection of illustrations can be of assistance to model builders, carriage restorers and artists, the captions include, where available, notes on finish and trimmings, along with a few basic dimensions to convey scale. A far wider range of colors was employed by the wagon builder than by the carriage builder; multicolor striping was also more commonly used, along with all sorts of elaborate decorations.

Although the plates in this book are generally accurate scale drawings, some carriage draftsmen, to simplify their drawings, decreased the number of spokes of wheels shown. In actuality, front wheels usually had 12 spokes; rear wheels 14. It may seem surprising that many lighter carriage wheels had two more spokes per wheel, but this was necessary since the lighter felloes require support more frequently. Wagon wheels up to about 42–44 inches usually have 12 spokes; above that, 14. Smaller wheels may have two spokes less per wheel, while those carrying heavier loads may have 14 front and 16 rear or, occasionally, the same number in front and rear. Some judgment in needed to determine the correct number. For example, no. 20 shows ten and 12 spokes, but this should be 12 and 14, since the load was relatively heavy. Likewise, no. 25 shows eight and ten—also too light, and better increased to ten and 12. No. 191, on the other hand, shows a smaller vehicle that carried a comparatively light load on smaller wheels, so that eight and ten may have been acceptable, yet ten and 12 might have been better. The wheels shown in many illustrations should be carefully considered, and the number of spokes based on diameter, weight carried and felloe cross section.

GLOSSARY

Apron. A piece of leather, enameled cloth or rubber cloth, attached to the dash or front of the carriage, used as a lap cover to protect the occupants from rain or snow.

Axle. A transverse bar of wood or metal forming the shaft on which a pair of wheels revolves. The ends of the axle that fit into the wheel hubs are known as axle arms, while the part between the arms is known as the axle bed.

Axle, cranked or dropped. An axle with a bed made after the fashion of a crank, so that the body of the vehicle may be hung lower.

Axle, dead. A term indicating that a vehicle body is mounted directly on the running gear without using springs.

Bob. A short sled, used with another of the same type, to carry a vehicle body, forming, as it were, the front and rear axle assemblies. The front bob turns around a kingbolt, and often has a fifth wheel. While a short body can be used with a single pair of runners, bobs are used to accommodate longer bodies.

Body irons. Any of the iron fittings of a body that brace, reinforce or support wooden parts.

Bolster. A wooden support for the body of a wagon that is made without springs. It resembles an axle bed, and is mounted above the axle.

Boot. A term having a variety of meanings in carriage usage. Originally, it was applied to a box, on the front or rear of a vehicle, that carried luggage. Eventually it came to be applied to the support for some driving seats. On certain types of farm wagons it was a small box projecting beyond the rear of the body, serving as a place to stand while shoveling grain, etc.

Bracket. A wooden or, more usually, a metal part used to carry, brace or support some other part. It may carry a separate part, such as a loading skid.

Brake. A mechanism for retarding or arresting the motion of a vehicle by friction. The principal parts are: the lever, by which the force is applied; the beam, which carries the shoes; the shoes, which come in contact with the rims of the wheels; and the rods, which transmit the motion of the lever to the beam. On some vehicles, the lever is actually a pedal.

Breeching. The part of a harness that encircles the breech of a horse, enabling the animal to retard or back the vehicle.

Camel-back top. A fixed top covering the entire length of a delivery wagon, rising in a hump over the driver's seat.

Carriage knob. A small metal knob, resembling a capstan in shape. Made to be screwed, driven or riveted in place, it is used to secure curtains or straps.

Chamfers. Beveled edges of parts.

Clerestory. A wall, raised above an adjoining roof, pierced with windows to admit air and light, such as the clerestory on the roof of an omnibus or railway car.

Clip. A piece of metal having a flat center, the ends being left round, upon which screw threads are cut; a U-bolt, having a wide, flat center. The clip eliminates the necessity of boring a hole for an ordinary bolt, which weakens the parts to be united.

Coupling pole. The wooden pole that connects the front and rear parts of a wagon's running gear.

Cut-under. An arch or opening in the underside of a vehicle body that allows the front wheels to turn under the body, facilitating sharper turning of the vehicle in crowded areas.

Dash. A panel standing on the front of a vehicle to protect the occupants of the front seat from mud or water that may be thrown by the horses' feet. Usually a leather-covered iron frame, it is sometimes of wood, especially in the case of commercial vehicles.

Doubletree. Also called an evener, this is the movable front crossbar of a pair-horse vehicle. It is secured by a center bolt on which it swivels, the singletrees hanging from the ends.

Drop-center. A term applied to either an axle or a body. The drop-center axle allows the body to be lowered, while the drop-center body, such as in a bakery or milk wagon, allows easier access for the driver by lowering his compartment.

Drop tongue. A tongue fitted between a second pair of short hounds (side bars), pivoted between the principal hounds, allowing the tongue to drop when not in use, or to yield slightly on an uneven roadway.

Endgate. The back end of a wagon body, hinged or otherwise, attached to the bottom in such a way that it can be dropped or removed for convenience in loading and unloading.

Felloe. A sawed or bentwood segment of a wheel rim.

Fifth wheel. A horizontal metal circle, or section of a circle, placed between the body and front axle of a vehicle, and generally connected to both by a kingbolt. It allows the axle to turn and change the line of motion without disturbing the balance of the body.

Flareboard. An extra board, flaring outward at the top, attached to the top of a wagon box to increase the carrying capacity.

Footboard. The footrest for the driver. It also serves as a dash, when no upright dash is used.

Garden seat. A seating arrangement, used on the upper deck of a double-deck omnibus, in which all seats face forward, with a central aisle.

Gear (or running gear). The underpart or running part of a vehicle, including axles, springs, fifth wheel, wheels, etc.

Hames. Curved pieces of wood or metal fitted to a horse collar, against which a horse bears to draw a vehicle.

Hammercloth. An ornamental valance on a driving seat.

Hammer pin. A doubletree pin with a head in the form of a hammer, allowing it to be used as a tool as well as a pin.

Hub runner. A sled runner made to fit onto an axle arm of a wheeled vehicle, a set of which converts the vehicle into a sled or sleigh for winter use.

Knees. Erect wooden supports running upward from the runners of a sleigh or sled.

Knifeboard seat. A seating arrangement, used on the upper deck of a double-deck omnibus, in which long benches, placed back-to-back, extend the length of the bus.

Lamp. A vehicle's lantern, attached to a seat, boot, body or dash.

Lazy board. A small board projecting from under the left side of a wagon (such as a Conestoga or other freight wagon), near the center, on which the driver could ride, and from which he could operate both the jerk line and the brake.

Light. A carriage or wagon window.

Line, jerk. A single line used for driving four or more horses. It is attached to a ring near the center of the lead rein on the near leader. The horse is turned to the left by a steady pull, and to the right by a number of quick jerks.

Lines, double. Driving by means of a separate line to each side of the bit, as opposed to jerk-line driving.

Nave. An old term for hub, more commonly used in England.

Patent wheel. A wheel employing some patented feature. Most commonly, the hub was the patented part, being strengthened by malleable iron fittings. The two most common wheels were the Sarven and Warner.

Perch. A piece of timber or a bar of iron or steel that connects the front and rear portions of a running gear.

Pillar. The general name for any piece of upright framework in a carriage body.

Pole. See tongue.

Rail. A slender wooden member used in the construction of a vehicle body, usually running the length or width of the body.

Rave. A horizontal rail in a wagon body, usually on the side of the vehicle. Also, a longitudinal piece above the knees of a sled, joining with the runner in front.

Rub iron. An iron plate on the side of a body or gear that protects the area from being worn by the front wheel.

Seat riser. A wood or metal support that elevates a seat above the body of a wagon.

Shafts. The pair of wooden poles, between which the horse is secured for the purpose of draft.

Sideboard. A board attached to the top of a wagon body to increase the carrying capacity.

Skid. An iron box placed under the wheel of a vehicle. Attached to the vehicle by a chain, it prevents the wheel from turning while the vehicle is going down a hill. It is used when the road is too steep or slippery to depend on the brake alone.

Spring, bolster. A spring, either leaf or coil, placed between the bolster and body of an otherwise unsuspended vehicle.

Spring, elliptic. A popular carriage spring, invented in 1804, in which two sets of overlapping steel leaves are hinged together at the ends, the general form being an acute ellipse.

Spring, platform. A combination of leaf springs designed to bring the body as near as possible to the axle. The most common form uses two three-quarter elliptics, the rear ends of which are joined by a cross-spring.

Spring, truck. A heavy half-elliptic spring used on a truck. The front end is shackled to the body, but the unshackled rear end slides in a box.

Stakes. Upright members framed into bolsters to retain the wagon body, or members framed into the body to retain the load.

Stay chains. A pair of short chains, leading from the front axle to two points near the ends of the doubletree, that prevent excessive movement of the doubletree.

Steering knuckles. The fittings that carry the axle arms for the front wheels in an uncommon type of articulated carriage steering in which the front axle is fixed. They also have arms to which the steering linkage is connected. This became common in automotive design.

Thoroughbraces. An early form of vehicle suspension, used to the end of the carriage era in such vehicles as the Concord coach and some light wagons. The body of the vehicle is suspended on heavy leather straps, running the length of the body, that are attached to shackles or jacks at the ends of the running gear.

Tongue. A long timber extending from the front of a running gear. Extending between the wheel horses, it is used as a lever to guide the vehicle, and also to assist in braking or backing the vehicle.

Turnbuckle. An iron fitting, having both right- and left-handed threads, used to adjust the length of a rod, cable or thoroughbrace.

Wear strips. Wood or metal strips placed on the vehicle to protect a surface from wear. Examples are wooden strips placed on a roof to protect the roof fabric from luggage carried there, or the iron strips on the back of a vehicle to protect from luggage on a rear rack.

Wheelhouse. See cut-under.

Whiffletree. A bar of wood or iron, pivoted at its center to the center of the crossbar, to which the traces are attached.

1. Dumpcart. This convenient, highly maneuverable vehicle was popular with farmers, contractors and anyone handling materials that could be dumped. A simple catch at the front end of the body could be released, and the body, which was pivoted under the center, dumped backward by hand. The cart shown here could carry 1700 pounds. A common color scheme was a blue body on either a red or yellow gear. Wheels 54". Studebaker Bros. Mfg. Co., South Bend, Indiana, catalog no. 222, 1903, p. 56.

2. Peerless dumpcart. Intended principally for city coal deliv- ery, this cart was considerably more complicated and expensive than no. 1. To keep the horse from standing crosswise in the street, the cart was designed to be drawn up parallel to the curb. A crank was turned to elevate the body above the wheels by means of chains. The body was turned 90 degrees, the rear end toward the sidewalk, a chute was attached under a small door and the coal was dumped into the basement without spillage onto the sidewalk. This cart was patented and built by William Leonhardt, a wagon builder of Baltimore. Medium blue body, striped white. Dark vermilion gear, striped black, edged with white. Wheels 62". *The Hub,* vol. 25, Oct. 1883, pl. 61.

3

4

3. **Ox cart.** This sturdy dumpcart has a pole instead of shafts, for it was designed for use with a team of oxen. Weighing twice as much as the average one-horse dumpcart, it could carry more than twice the load. Since the loads of carts were distributed on only two wheels, and since they often ran on soft ground, the wheels frequently had tires that were 4″ or more in width. Wheels 60″. R. H. Allen & Co., New York City, catalog of ca. 1883, p. 215.

4. **Garbage cart.** Some carts were built for special purposes. This 300-gallon dumping garbage cart had a watertight steel body that insured sanitation by preventing the foul-smelling drippings from wet garbage from running out onto the street. Haywood Wagon Co., Newark, New York, catalog of ca. 1910, p. 35.

5

6

5. Dray cart. Termed either a dray or a truck, according to the whim of the user, these simple two-wheelers were among the major vehicles of the eighteenth and nineteenth centuries. Used extensively by business and industry, countless early sketches and paintings of street scenes testify to their importance. More common than four-wheelers in the eighteenth century, they carried lumber, barrels, boxes, bales and all sorts of merchandise. The illustration on this New York billhead presents them in a mid-nineteenth-century setting. (Original document in the Smithsonian Institution.)

6. Dray cart. The cart was usually made without a floor. The loads, resting on the cross members of the frame, were retained by stakes. Two permanently attached skids protruded from the rear of the vehicle. When the horse was harnessed to the cart, the shafts were slightly elevated and the skids consequently almost touched the ground, making it easier to slide or roll loads onto the vehicle. The illustration shows a heavy casting on a dray at the Port Richmond Iron Works in Philadelphia around the 1850s. A number of other drays can be seen in the background. (Lithograph by I. P. Morris & Co., in the Smithsonian Institution.)

7

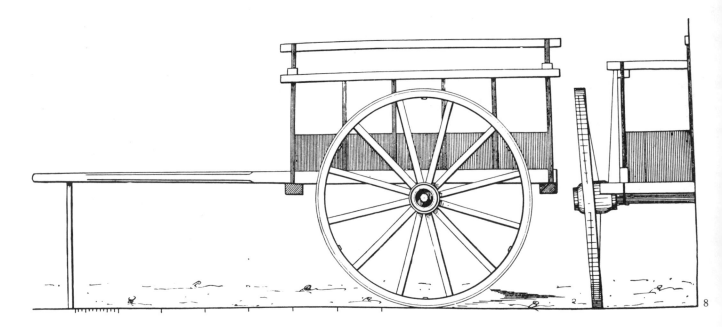

8

7. Dray cart. While many of these carts were never painted, this one was probably tastefully painted. It was also improved by the addition of springs, lacking in earlier models. As the nineteenth century progressed, the two-wheeler was increasingly replaced by the four-wheeler, yet some of the two-wheel drays served side by side with the motortruck well into the twentieth century. R. H. Allen & Co., New York City, catalog of ca. 1883, p. 219.

8. Red River cart. For more than three-quarters of a century from 1800, the settlers of the Red River area of the United States and Canada used these rude carts both as personal vehicles and as freighters. As the latter, generally unpainted, they carried trading goods to such places as St. Paul, Minnesota. Entirely of wood, lacking even iron tires, they also omitted the center rail, shown here, which supported a cloth or skin cover. This lighter version was better-finished for personal use and did boast tires. Black body on a red gear, striped black. Some also had red and yellow decorations. Wheels 56″. *The Hub,* vol. 24, Aug. 1882, pl. 52.

9

10

9. Red River carts. This Frederic Remington drawing shows a procession of carts on the way to market. Thin wood strips can be seen where rawhide binds them over the felloe joints of the unshod wheels. Some of the harnesses use breast collars while others use round collars. An original Red River harness, of rawhide, in the collections of the Smithsonian Institution, is equipped with the round collar. Instead of the separate collar and hames, the simple wood hames have grass-stuffed canvas pads tacked to the rear sides.

10. Piano truck. Here is a special-purpose two-wheeler, expressly made to deliver pianos. Platform springs protect the heavy, though fragile, load (two-piano capacity) from severe jolts. The driver could have his seat in place only when the vehicle was empty; when it was loaded, he had to stand. Dark green body striped white. Carmine gear, striped black with fine white lines. Wheels 38″. *The Hub,* vol. 30, May 1888, pl. 17.

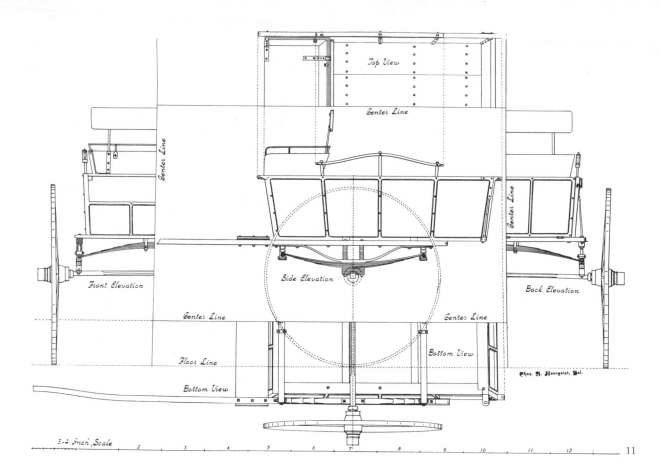

11. Business cart. This open delivery cart is of a more refined construction than most. Both sides and ends flare, and the short, curved top rail is both functional and decorative. The driving seat slides backward and forward to balance the cart when loaded or unloaded. As shown, the cart would have been loaded, and when empty, the seat would have been moved backward. Wheels 50″. *The Carriage Monthly,* vol. 39, Nov. 1903.

12. Milk cart. Made to service a more affluent neighborhood, this cart was intended more to impress than to function efficiently. The driving seat, borrowed from Hansom cab design, had the opposite effect of the drop-center milk wagon, creating a hardship on the driver. The milk bottles were packed in ice, in zinc boxes. The cart was built by Robert Jones, of Brooklyn, New York. Dark green body. Black moldings striped red and gold. Yellow gear, striped black. Silver-plated mountings. Wheels 52″. *The Hub,* vol. 33, Oct. 1891, pl. 44.

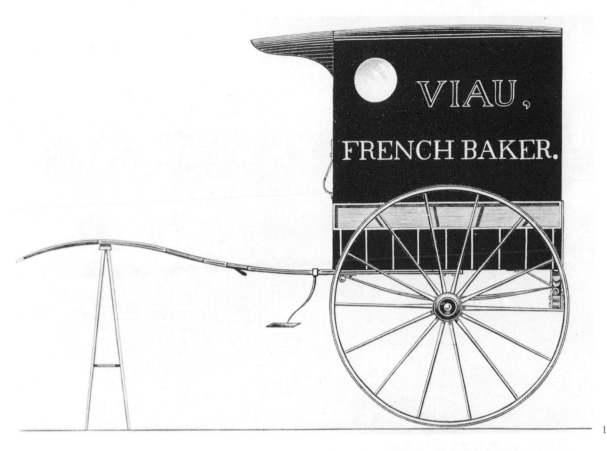

13

14

13. Baker's cart. Closed carts without a dash were popular with shops making light deliveries. Colorfully finished, the lower panels were light blue, the center panels were light vermilion and the upper panels and moldings were black. Light vermilion gear, striped black. Wheels 53″. *The Hub,* vol. 22, Nov. 1880, pl. 82.

14. Parcel-delivery cart. A more common style of cart featured the conventional leather-covered dash. This one also carries lamps, a refinement many carts lacked. Those of the finer quality also had beveled-glass windows. Dark green lower body panels. Black upper panels and moldings, with a fine line of gold between the moldings. Dark vermilion gear, striped black. Green leather trimmings. Silver or brass mountings. Wheels 51″. *The Hub,* vol. 25, Dec. 1883, pl. 76.

15

16

15. Bandwagon. Not all bands were marching bands; some villages, lodges and factories had bands that rode in wagons such as this one. In an era of limited travel and entertainment, small bands were more common than they are now, and their frequent performances were eagerly awaited by the public. The body of this wagon was dark green with gold scrollwork that was omitted from this drawing. Naples yellow gear, striped blue and gold. Dark green goatskin trimming. Wheels 42½″ and 55″. *The Carriage Monthly,* vol. 17, Dec. 1881, pl. 76.

16. Circus bandwagon. The style of circus bandwagons was entirely different from village bandwagons, for the intention was to be gaudy. The musicians sat at a considerable height, and there were usually compartments under the floor for storage of the instruments. This wagon was built by the Schultz Wagon

Co. of Dalton, Ohio. The body and gear were white. The figures were painted many colors, and gold leaf was freely used on the scrolls. Striping of the gear was heavy and ornate. Wheels 40″ and 52″. *The Carriage Monthly,* vol. 30, Jan. 1895, pl. 59.

17. Freight wagon. This gigantic wagon was built for the Fortuna Mining Co., of Yuma County, Arizona, by M. P. Henderson & Son, of Stockton, California, who were famous for their Western stage wagons. It weighed 6515 pounds and carried 12 tons. The wheels measured 5′ and 8′ with 16″ and 20″ hubs, 4⅝″ spokes, and 1″ × 6″ tires. The rear wheels are said to have weighed 1800 pounds each. The bed measured 20′ × 5′, with a standard width of 44″. Unfortunately, the number of horses required to draw the wagon is not given. *The Carriage Monthly,* vol. 35, Nov. 1899, p. 285.

18

19

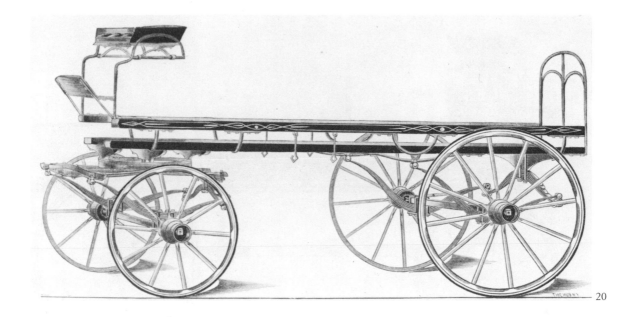

18. **Truck.** Exceeding the Fortuna freight wagon in size is this giant truck, named Thunder, built by J. A. Shephard & Sons of New York City. Intended to move large machinery, castings, huge blocks of stone, etc., it was so large that it had to be built in the street, in front of the Shephard shops. The main beams were 14″ × 16″, and the tires were 1½″ × 9″. Wheel diameter is not given, but the hubs were 24″, and the wheels weighed 3000 pounds each. The seven-ton vehicle required six horses to move it when empty, and it was estimated that 50 would be required for a full load. Since this was a city vehicle, one wonders how well a 50-horse team negotiated city streets. *The Carriage Monthly,* vol. 29, Jan. 1894, p. 315.

19. **Brewer's truck.** Vehicles used by the brewing industry were, contrary to popular belief, not all of one type; there was a variety of trucks, drays, express wagons and delivery wagons. One of the more picturesque styles was the truck, modified slightly to make it adaptable to bulk delivery in kegs. Here is a heavy brewer's truck of about 1900, built by William Schukraft & Sons, Chicago. The eight hooks hanging underneath carried four additional kegs. (Photograph from the Smithsonian Institution.)

20. **Brewer's truck.** This is a medium-size truck for keg delivery. Platform springs were the usual suspension for this type of vehicle. Blue body, striped yellow. Yellow gear, striped black. Black-enameled duck seat cushion. Wheels 38″ and 48″. *The Hub,* vol. 26, March 1885, pl. 100.

21. **Brewer's wagon.** The express wagon, with its flareboards, was readily adaptable to the delivery of keg beer. Here is one of five-ton capacity by a famous builder of commercial vehicles in New York City, the Sebastian Wagon Co. Vermilion body, striped black with fine white lines. Yellow gear, striped black with fine red lines. Cushion and top of heavy canvas. Wheels 38″ and 54″. *The Hub,* vol. 36, Nov. 1894, pl. 120.

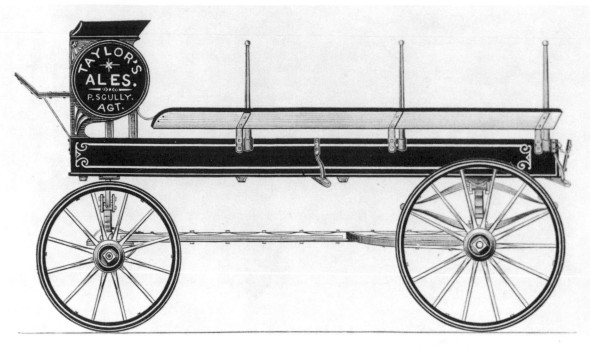

22. Brewer's wagon. Barely large enough to qualify as an express wagon, this is hardly more than an open three-spring delivery wagon with flareboards and express-type seat added, the last being embellished with a simulated keg. It was built by J. Weber, of Schenectady, New York. Dark green body, striped black with fine vermilion lines and gold lettering. Dark lake gear, striped black with fine white lines. Wheels 36″ and 42″. *The Hub,* vol. 22, June 1880, pl. 35.

23. Bottler's wagon. Beer was also delivered in bottles. Wagons carrying them were generally of lighter construction and were in the delivery-wagon class. Suspension could be on platform or elliptic springs, or a combination of the two. Here is a particularly attractive light delivery with cut-under body, showing bottle delivery in baskets. Blue body and gear, striped lighter blue. The handles were silver-plated. Wheels 39″ and 48″. *The Carriage Monthly,* vol. 26, Apr. 1890, pl. 8.

24. Bottler's wagon. This panel-body afforded enclosed delivery of bottles, except for the few boxes carried on top. Capacity was 33 to 35 boxes, each holding 24 bottles. The body was paneled both inside and outside the framework, so that insulation, composed of charcoal dust, could be installed to help prevent excessive heating of the beer. The inside was lined with zinc. Milori green body. Light vermilion center panel, with gold-lettering. Chrome yellow gear, striped black with a fine line of red. Black leather trimming. Brass mountings. Wheels 35″ and 48″. *The Hub,* vol. 25, Sept. 1883, pl. 53.

25. Hearse. Used to convey the coffin to the grave site, the hearse was finely built and elegantly finished and decorated. Traditionally black, usually without striping, its somber aspect was offset by the high degree of ornamentation, which sometimes came close to exceeding the limit of good taste. This early example, decorated with carvings and plumes, is rather ordinary. Wheels 37″ and 46″. *The Coach-makers' Illustrated Magazine,* vol. 2, Aug. 1856, fig. 44.

26

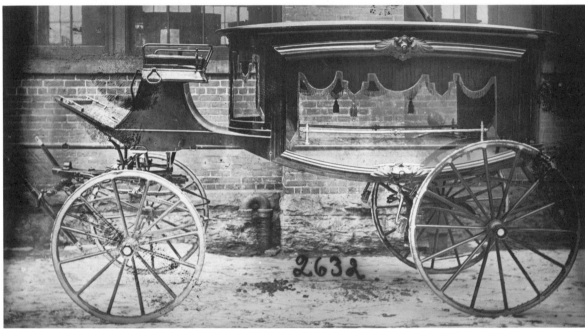

27

26. Hearse. Here is a dignified example, with a body of an unusual design that somewhat resembles an altar. A hammercloth, borrowed from coach design, ornaments the driving seat. Doors, as usual, are at the rear, and inside are the draperies of mourning. The floors of hearses had small rollers to assist in loading and unloading, and various devices to hold the coffin in place. Body and gear, the customary black, with the interior painted to imitate dark rosewood. Wheels 40″ and 49″. *The Hub,* vol. 25, Aug. 1883, color pl. 20.

27. Hearse. This is a typical example of late-nineteenth-century hearse, but the brakes, not a customary feature, suggest it was built for a hilly area. Inside are mourning draperies and plated railings. The only other devices are the ornaments on the window moldings. This tasteful vehicle is from the shops of James Cunningham, Son & Co., of Rochester, New York, the famed builders of hearses and fine carriages. Because hearses were well built, received light and limited usage and were well cared for, a significant number have survived. (Cunningham photograph from the Smithsonian Institution.)

28. Hearse. An elegant and expensive hearse of an ordinary style, except that it carries draperies of mourning on the outside. The outer cloth was black, with a silver-gray lining showing at the edges. The underdrapery was almost black, with just enough of a tinge of purple to be noticeable. It was built by another famed hearse builder, The Crane and Breed Mfg. Co., of Cincinnati, Ohio. All black, unstriped, with brass mountings. Wheels 38½″ and 50″. *The Carriage Monthly,* vol. 34, June 1898, pl. 12.

29. Hearse. Another elegant style by James Cunningham, Son & Co. Richly ornamented with extensive carving, plated urns and massive lamps, this carriage maintains its dignity. Less-expensive hearses by lesser-known builders often lost this dignity by overornamentation with cheap, almost gaudy, devices. Many early motor hearses were nothing more than horse-drawn bodies placed on motortruck chassis. (Cunningham photograph from the Smithsonian Institution.)

28

29

30

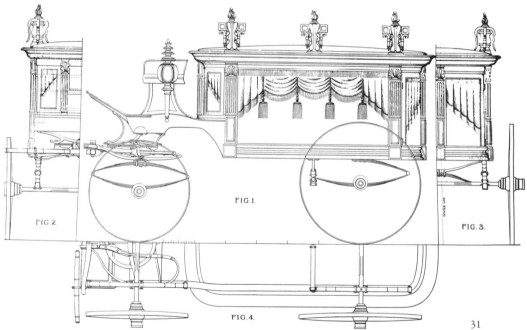

FIG.1.

FIG.2.

FIG.3.

FIG.4.

31

30. Hearse. Here is a hearse of hearses built by Cunningham for exhibition at the World's Columbian Exposition of 1893. Few other vehicles ever surpassed this one. The interior was finished in mahogany; mountings were of silver. The carved spokes were an unusual feature in the United States. In view of the high survival rate of hearses, one wonders if this one could, perhaps, still exist. All black, some parts being given a flat finish for contrast. Wheels 40″ and 48″. *The Carriage Monthly,* vol. 29, June 1893, pl. 19.

31. Child's hearse. While hearses for adults were traditionally black, those for children were white. Some were slightly smaller; others were nearly full-size. H. Duhamel, of Brooklyn, New York, built this typical child's hearse. While it was the usual white, the pillars and top urns were black. The draperies were of black, white and purple broadcloth, and the driving cushion was of white leather. Wheels 36″ and 46″. *The Hub,* vol. 41, Aug. 1899, p. 172.

32

33

32. Child's hearse. An unusual combination of a child's hearse with a coupé permitted the parents to ride with the body of their child. The portion containing the casket pivoted 90 degrees, and there were the conventional rear double doors, so that the casket could be removed in the ordinary manner. The entire vehicle was white, striped gold, and the mountings were gold-finished. Trimmings were drab corduroy. Wheels 36" and 44". *The Hub,* vol. 31, Aug. 1889, pl. 34.

33. Infant hearse. A rare combination by Cunningham joins a small hearse body, which doubles as a driving seat, with the body of a coach. This permits either the family or pallbearers to ride with the deceased infant. All white; the gear is striped, probably gold, edged with black. The hearse body could be detached and a conventional driving seat substituted, in which instance the coach could be used to accompany a child's hearse in a funeral procession. (Cunningham photograph from the Smithsonian Institution.)

17

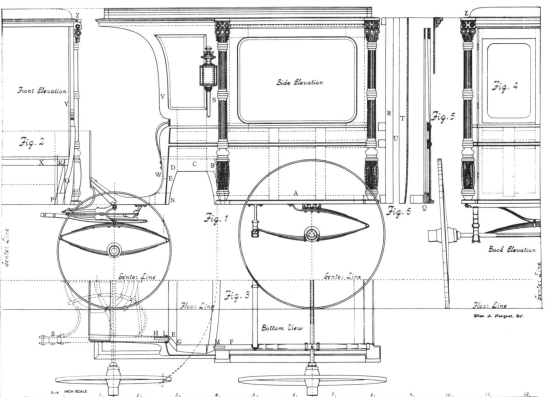

34. Undertaker's wagon. These vehicles, built in the style of delivery wagons, were variously used to carry caskets and other funeral accessories at times other than funeral processions, and to carry flowers in a procession. They were as finely finished as a hearse, in the traditional black; the restrained use of striping was acceptable. Open wagons such as this one were common in the earlier period. The moldings of this wagon were silver leaf, and the wheels were striped with fine white lines. Wheels 42"

and 50". *The Hub,* vol. 22, Feb. 1881, pl. 124.

35. Undertaker's wagon. By the 1890s the enclosed style had nearly replaced the open wagon. This is nothing more than a delivery wagon with hearse-style carvings. Black, the gear striped dark green. Trimmings of dark green cloth. Wheels 35" and 42". *The Carriage Monthly,* vol. 34, Oct. 1898, p. 201.

36

37

36. Undertaker's wagon. An expensive example from the famous Cunningham shops, this one is longer than many, Dating from about 1900, it rolls on solid-rubber tires. These wagons frequently had folding racks inside, so that flowers could be carried on two levels. Draperies were permanently hung between the outer glass and an inside panel. (Cunningham photograph from Smithsonian Institution.)

37. Ambulance. The usual ambulance design was, like that of so many special-purpose vehicles, patterned after the enclosed delivery wagon. This Studebaker is a typical example. Inside was a basket stretcher equipped with a rubber-covered mattress and an air pillow, and an attendant's chair that folded out of the way. The entire interior had a natural-wood finish; the floor was covered with oilcloth. Most ambulances had a warning bell; some had brakes, as does this one. Black body on a red or green gear, striped black. Leather trimmings. Wheels 33" and 45". List price $1010. Studebaker Bros. Mfg. Co., South Bend, Indiana, catalog no. 601, 1912, p. 114.

38. Ambulance. An offering of another famous builder of commercial vehicles, Fulton and Walker, of Philadelphia, this ambulance has a drop-center that resembles a rockaway carriage, providing easy access for the attendant, who has a seat alongside the patient. Like most ambulances, it has the cut-under feature to allow sharp turning in crowded areas. Deep green body with black moldings, striped olive green. Deep green gear, striped olive green. Wheels 37″ and 50″. *The Carriage Monthly,* vol. 35, Nov. 1899, pl. 189.

39. Ambulance. James Cunningham, Son & Co. built many vehicles besides hearses, all of them elegant. This ambulance has side doors for the convenience of attendants, rubber tires for the comfort of all occupants, leaded beveled-glass windows and ventilating louvers. Colors are not known, but the following would have been appropriate: black body with lower panels, bracket front and pillars of deep blue; deep blue gear, striped white. Trimmings of black leather. (Cunningham photograph, ca. 1900, from the Smithsonian Institution.)

40

40. Ambulance interior. This shows the inside of the ambulance illustrated in no. 39. It carries two stretchers and a folding attendant's seat. The hanging stretcher is suspended on coil springs; a water tank can be seen in the upper right front corner. In front is an upholstered seat for additional attendants, or injured patients who are able to walk. Three windows open in front, two in the doors and two in the rear, to offer ample ventilation in summer. There are probably some small compartments in front for medical supplies, for the Cunninghams left little to be desired. (Cunningham photograph from the Smithsonian Institution.)

41

42

41. Army ambulance. Developed by Brigadier General D. H. Rucker, and initially built in the government repair shops in Washington, the Rucker ambulance saw extensive use during the latter part of the Civil War. Its four litters—two on the floor, two above them—could be arranged to form seats along both sides for the walking wounded. Water, for drinking and for medical purposes, was contained in a keg under the driver's seat. *Medical & Surgical History of the War of the Rebellion,* Surgical vol. 3, p. 952, Washington, Gov't. Printing Office, 1883.

42. Army ambulance. During the 1870s, the Army worked to develop a new ambulance design; the Secretary of War approved this one in 1881. It had spring-supported rollers on the floor to hold the litters, and the body of the vehicle was on platform springs. If walking wounded were carried, the litters folded out of the way, and benches were pulled up along both sides. For ease in shipping, the bows could be removed and the sides folded down on a level with the middle rail. *Specifications for Means of Transportation,* Washington, Gov't. Printing Office, 1882.

43

44

43. Veterinary ambulance. Animals, especially horses and mules, on occasion required treatment, so special ambulances were designed for them. In this vehicle, a cranked axle lowered the floor, and a high, sturdy endgate formed a ramp when lowered. After the animal was led in, a heavy canvas sling was passed under it and drawn up tight for support by ratchet-equipped rollers. Deep green body and chamfers with black posts, pillars, top rails, bottom rails and boot. Deep green gear, striped black. Wheels 38″ and 46″. *The Carriage Monthly,* vol. 34, Aug. 1898, pl. 25.

44. Veterinary ambulance. Similar in operation to the four-wheel version is this Army two-wheeler, ca. 1917–18. The endgate is shown lowered for loading. The bottom of the endgate has stops to prevent the card from tipping backward when being loaded with a heavy burden. Note the side location of the driver's seat and the foot-operated brake. (U.S. Army photograph from the Smithsonian Institution.)

45. Gypsy wagon. One of the better-known types of living quarters on wheels was the gypsy wagon. Necessarily compact, it made ingenious use of all available space; there were often many compartments, some hidden, for storage of all sorts of items. Larger furniture, such as beds and tables, usually folded out of the way when not in use. For heating and cooking, some wagons had stoves, others had open fireplaces. Decoration was gaudy and ornate, with bright colors and often much gold and silver leaf. This wagon was built by T. Cook and Bros., of Chester, Pennsylvania, a firm that made a specialty of the type. *The Carriage Monthly,* vol. 38, Aug. 1902, pl. 625.

46. Sheep wagon. These wagons were the living quarters of Western sheepherders from the mid-1880s onward. Basically, the design was that of a modified farm wagon. Wide shelves, extending outward, were attached to the tops of the sides to form benches. It also contained a bed, table and stove. An outside box, attached to one side of the wagon, stored food supplies and was accessible from inside the wagon. The top was covered with canvas, but was frequently lined inside with blankets, linoleum or sheet metal. Studebaker Bros. Mfg. Co., South Bend, Indiana, catalog no. 222, 1903, p. 41.

47. Camping wagon. Similar in design to a sheep wagon, the camper's wagon could be built on a farm wagon or an open delivery wagon. Boxes for storage of supplies and equipment could be constructed on top of the benches, as shown. Other conveniences could be provided according to the ingenuity of the builder or customer. The drawing shows a feedbox for horses on the rear of the wagon body. *The Blacksmith and Wheelwright,* Apr. 1902, p. 162.

46

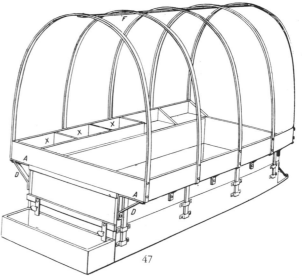

47

48

49

48. Peddler's wagon. Itinerant peddlers traveled from village to village, stopping at all the homes along the road. Many traveled far from their homes and were gone for long periods of time. As they became more experienced, they could anticipate where their stock would begin to run low, and made prior arrangements to have small shipments arrive at the various rail depots on their route to replenish it. This attractive wagon has a Chinese vermilion body on a straw-color gear, both striped black. Wheels 42″ and 50″. *The New York Coachmaker's Magazine,* vol. 2, Nov. 1859, pl. 20.

49. Peddler's wagon. A most efficient wagon, this makes full use of every available bit of space. The sides open, exposing sliding trays. There are additional compartments under the footboards, and under and behind the seat. Boxes of goods could also be carried on top, within the railing and on the rear luggage rack. Tinware was a popular line, but a variety of small

household and novelty items, such as are found in five-and-ten stores, was generally stocked too. This wagon is in the Smithsonian collections. (Photograph from the Smithsonian Institution.)

50. Peddler's wagon. Another style of peddler's wagon was made for the local peddler, who did not go far from home, usually operating in his home city or in nearby villages. These wagons, small and well finished, were actually a variety of light business wagon. Doors were generally in the rear, and the items carried were limited to small merchandise such as perfume, patent medicine, stationery and sewing supplies. This one was by the famed builder of Concord coaches, the Abbot, Downing Co. Medium ultramarine blue body; drab or French gray roof and light area. Drab or French gray gear, striped blue. Dark blue morocco or enameled leather trimmings. Wheels 44″ and 48″. *The Hub,* vol. 22 Apr. 1880, pl. 9.

51

52

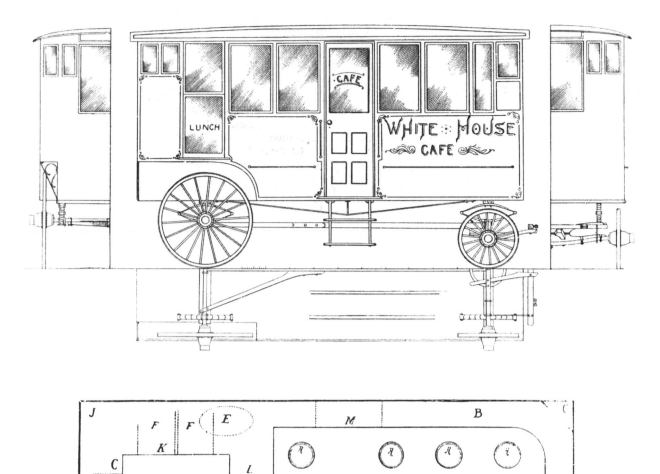

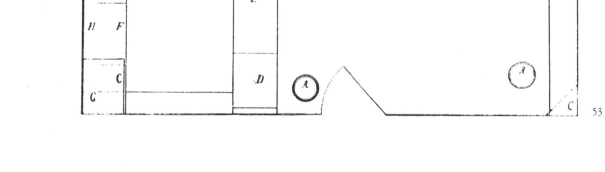

51. Peddler's wagon. These wagons could be painted gaudy colors, to attract attention, or they could be painted and lettered to suit the peddler's needs. This one happened to be rather subdued, for the suggestions were for a black body, or a dark green one with black moldings, on a yellow or carmine gear, striped black. Green cloth trimmings. The axle nuts were silver-plated, and if lamps were used, a silver finish was recommended for them as well. Wheels 37″ and 48″. *The Carriage Monthly,* vol. 28, Oct. 1892, pl. 54.

52. Lunch wagon. These large, vanlike vehicles were constructed to be used for serving light meals and refreshments, primarily to nightworkers; few restaurants stayed open all night, and these wagons could be drawn to the various places where there was a graveyard shift. This ornately painted example had an extremely light gear with only 28″ wheels, since it rarely had to be moved. An attractive, naturally

finished, veneered interior contained a counter, cupboard, drawers and shelves. *The Carriage Monthly,* vol. 32, Oct. 1896, pl. 37.

53. Lunch wagon. In New York, night lunch wagons were known as "The Owl." Customers could enter and sit on one of the stools (*A*) at the counter (*B*), or they could be served at the sidewalk from the window marked "Lunch." The windows were of colored glass, so that diners could avoid the gaze of passersby. The kitchen was equipped with an oil stove, coffee urn, sink, closets, shelves and drawers. A 16′ body was mounted on a substantial gear with 29″ and 48″ wheels, indicating that this one was expected to be moved about frequently. White body and gear, with red and gold striping and lettering; landscape scenes on sides and ends; cherry-finish interior. *The Hub,* vol. 36, June 1894, p. 176.

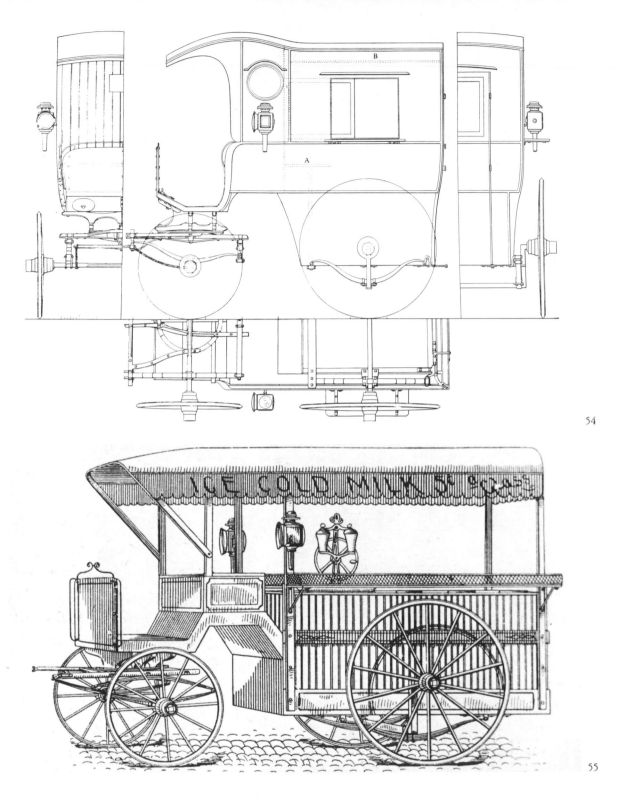

54

55

54. Coffee wagon. Serving coffee and sandwiches, this wagon was not intended for the public, but was part of a fleet operated by the City of New York to serve lunch to firemen and street-cleaning crews. The lower shelf (*A*) carried the coffee tank, while the upper shelves (*B*) stored cups and spoons. Outside the sliding windows were shelves for serving. A gong under the footboard alerted workers to refreshments. Maroon body and gear, striped yellow. Wheels 32″ and 44″. *The Hub,* vol. 45, Feb. 1904, p. 423.

55. Iced-milk wagon. While the larger wagons operated at night, a smaller variety served during the day, generally offering less than a complete lunch. A popular one was the iced-milk wagon, which, during the warm months, served buttermilk, sweet milk and milk shakes made of sweet milk and eggs. Some wagons also offered muffins. This wagon has a drop-center rear axle to allow the body enough depth for headroom. Ice tanks for the milk cans are along both sides; the hand-operated milk-shake machine can be seen in the rear. White body and gear, striped blue. Wheels 36″ and 48″. *The Hub,* vol. 36, June 1894, p. 177.

56

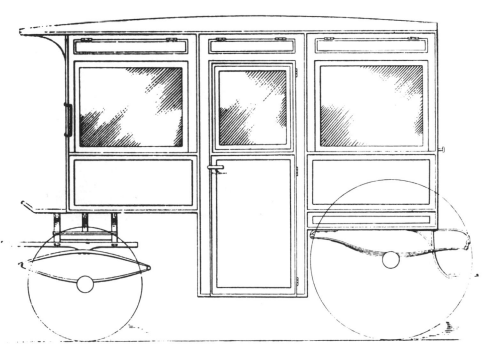

57

56. Waffle wagon. A less common vending wagon was this waffle wagon, which was something of a mobile kitchen, for it was equipped with an oil cooking stove and the necessary facilities for storage and mixing. In place of a drop-center rear axle, this wagon has the conventional straight axle, so that the operator had to step over a hump in the floor to get to the center of the wagon. Serving shelves run along the sides. *The Hub,* vol. 36, June 1894, p. 177.

57. Popcorn wagon. Another popular vending wagon was the popcorn wagon, which was used along busy thoroughfares, in such places as public parks and at sporting events. This one has fixed side windows, with hinged ventilators above them. The end lights are hinged at the top so that they swing inward and fasten to the roof. Popcorn was served from the rear window to customers standing on the long step. With the front light opened, the operator could sit outside to drive, or he could drive in a standing position from inside. Grained body on a light brown gear. Wheels 30″ and 43″. *The Hub,* vol. 36, June 1894, p. 186.

58. Farm wagon. In an era when the small farm played so significant a role in America's economy, few vehicles were of greater importance than the farm wagon. Built in countless small shops (later in large factories where they were mass-produced), its design was simple and utilitarian, amounting to a box on an unsprung running gear. Here is a typical light, one-horse wagon with a two-spring seat resting on the removable sideboards. Built by the E. D. Clapp Wagon Co., of Auburn, New York, this $50 wagon had a rated capacity of 1500 pounds. *The Hub,* vol. 23, Aug. 1881, p. 241.

59. Farm wagon. Varying slightly in design, this two-horse wagon by the E. D. Clapp Wagon Co. has flareboards instead of sideboards. While most farm wagons were unsprung, this one employs bolster springs between the body and the bolsters. The capacity was 5000 pounds. Light green body with yellow and white striping. Vermilion or straw-color gear. The decals were by the famous firm of Palm & Fechteler, of New York City, which introduced that form of decoration to the United States. Wheels 44″ and 54″. *The Hub,* vol. 23, July 1881, p. 186.

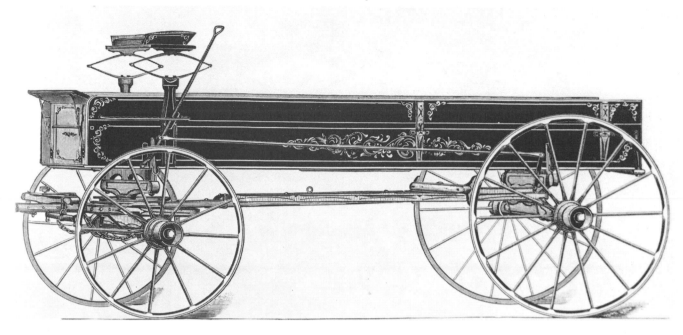

60

61

60. Farm wagon. This unusually long wagon had a seat on risers, instead of one resting on the body or sideboards. Like many farm wagons, it had wooden axles. Dark green body on an Indian red gear, striped black. Many of the earlier farm wagons lacked striping to save a small expense. Wheels 42″ and 51″. *The Carriage Monthly,* vol. 21, Jan. 1886, pl. 86.

61. Farm wagon. This beauty is anything but an ordinary farm wagon—it is a special show vehicle made by Studebaker for the World's Columbian Exposition of 1893. It was built of choice woods (the pole is of curly ash, the body is of rosewood with an inlaid border of holly). Also inlaid in the body are 35 medals awarded the company in earlier years. The tires are of steel, but all other metal parts are of polished aluminum, then a comparatively rare and expensive metal. It reportedly cost the company $2110.65 to build. The wagon survives in the Discovery Hall Museum at South Bend, Indiana. *The Hub,* vol. 35, July 1893, pl. 22.

62

63

62. Farm wagon. This is a typical late farm wagon, of which many examples survive. Mounted on steel axles, it was offered in four sizes with a capacity ranging from 2500 to 7000 pounds. Most of the larger farm wagons had brakes; this has a combination brake that can be operated from the driving seat, or, if an overhanging load of hay made that awkward, by the lever extending from the rear under the body. Columbia Wagon & Body Co., Columbia, Pennsylvania, catalog no. 53 of ca. 1908, p. 11.

63. Steel wheel. Early in the twentieth century, a number of farm wagons began to use all-steel wheels in place of the wood-spoke wheels. Empire Mfg. Co., Quincy, Illinois, catalog of ca. 1914, p. 6.

64. Grain wagon. Here is a special-purpose farm wagon made for areas where wheat or other grains were grown extensively. The deep body, with extensions running upward from the outer edges of the flareboards, made possible a variety of sizes ranging from 85- to 150-bushel capacity. Studebaker Bros. Mfg. Co., South Bend, Indiana, catalog no. 222, 1903, p. 51.

65. Hay wagon. The Enterprise Carriage and Wagon Works, of Morrisville, Pennsylvania, built this deep-bodied wagon to carry hay. Chrome yellow body, striped brown. Brown gear, striped chrome yellow. Wheels 46″ and 56″. *The Hub,* vol. 29, Sept. 1887, pl. 49.

66

67

68

69

66. Hay wagon. This peculiar but practical style of hay wagon was used in the Pennsylvania counties of Lancaster and Lebanon. Comparatively shallow in depth, the body has widely flaring sides, forming more of a tray than a box. Bodies, often 16′ or 18′ long, were loaded high and wide, with tall end racks securing the load from spilling over the ends. Capacities ranged from two to four tons. Columbia Wagon & Body Co., Columbia, Pennsylvania, catalog no. 53, ca. 1908, p. 20.

67. Round-up wagon. So-called by Studebaker, this wagon was also popularly known as a chuck wagon. Used on trail drives and for spring and fall roundups, it was the cook's center of operations. The drawers of the rear chest carried smaller utensils and food supplies; larger equipment and food stores were kept in front. The wagon also carried some trail equipment and camp gear. Studebaker Bros. Mfg. Co., South Bend, Indiana, catalog of 1887, p. 57.

68. Freight wagon. This is basically a farm wagon with an unusually deep body on a mountain gear—a powerful brake-leverage system coupled to a pair of very large brake shoes. The body was 12′ long and could be had in any depth from 36″ to 52″. These wagons were especially popular freight carriers in the West. The bow staples attached to the sides carried bows for a cover when desired. Studebaker Bros. Mfg. Co., South Bend, Indiana, catalog no. 222, 1903, p. 42.

69. Log wagon. Wagons intended for logging operations, needing no body, consisted of a running gear only. Logs were stacked on bunks, the heavy pieces of timber attached to the tops of the bolsters. Wheels were kept low, these being 41″ in front and rear to facilitate side-loading and unloading. The lever for the powerful brake protrudes over the coupling pole in the rear. Studebaker Bros. Mfg. Co., South Bend, Indiana, catalog no. 222, 1903. p. 45.

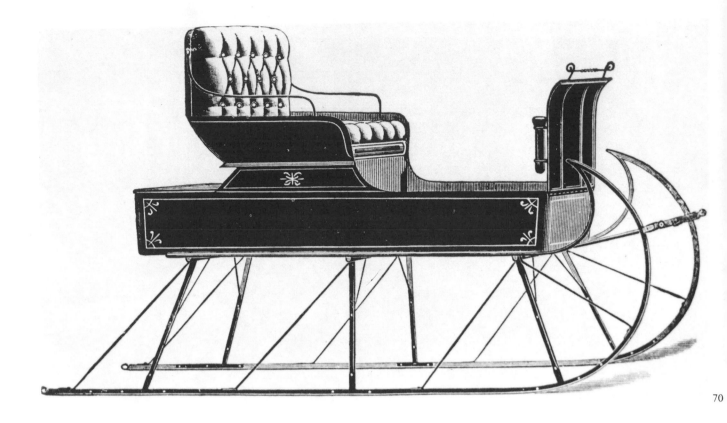

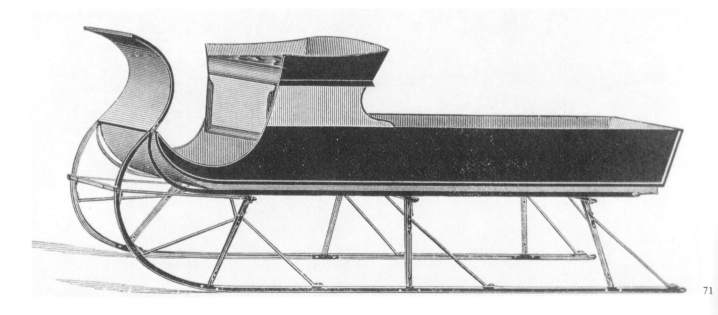

70. Business sled. There were many options for winter transportation: Special sleighs and sleds could be built; the body of a wheeled vehicle could be transferred onto runners; or hub runners could simply be substituted on the axles in place of wheels. Here is a light sled, capable of carrying a little more than a salesman's samples, in a body suggesting a piano-box buggy. *The Hub,* vol. 44, Aug. 1903, p. 191.

71. Business sled. Another small sled, capable of making deliveries of small parcels or packages, was simple, but attractively designed. It has a front end reminiscent of a Portland cutter. The body is 5'9" long from the front of the seat to the endgate. Lake body, striped gold. Light lake gear, striped red. *The Carriage Monthly,* vol. 16, July 1880, pl. 31.

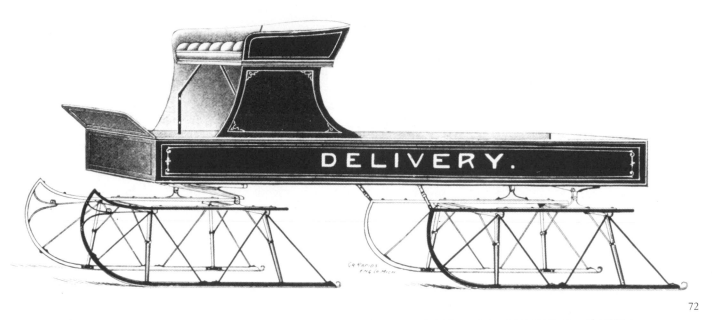

72

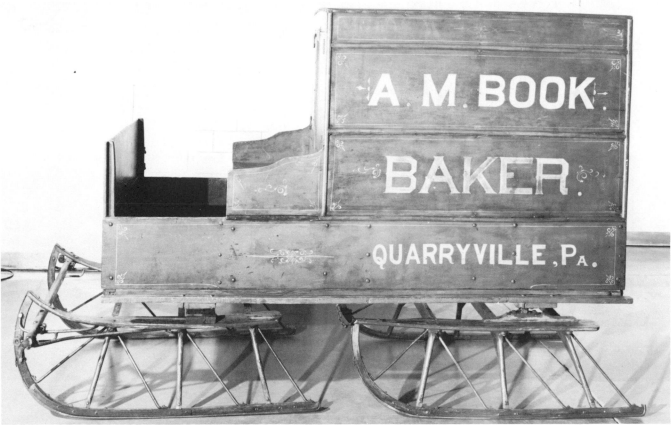

73

72. **Delivery sled.** As sleds become longer, it is more practical to have two sets of runners under them to facilitate turning and to render the entire unit less rigid when gliding over uneven surfaces. A most effective design attaches a pair of oscillating bobsleds, each unit being pivoted near its rear end, to the body. A pair of safety straps or chains at the front of the rear bob restricts excessive movement. Dimensions of the body shown above are 3'7" × 8'. Olive brown body on a light yellow or carmine gear. Sturtevant-Larrabee Co., Binghamton, New York, catalog of 1906–07, p. 53.

73. **Baker's sled.** Here is a primitive example of a body enclosed for better protection of fragile or perishable goods. It rests on a pair of oscillating bobs. Since there is no rear door, access to goods is gained through a pair of doors just behind the driver. One wonders if this was to prevent boys, aided by the sound-deadening quality of snow, from stealing pies when the sled was in motion. This sled, which operated about 1920, is deep red, striped yellow. (In the collection of the Smithsonian Institution.)

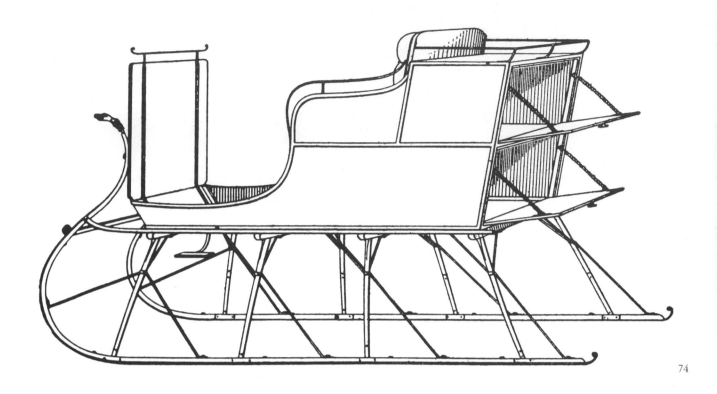

74

75

40

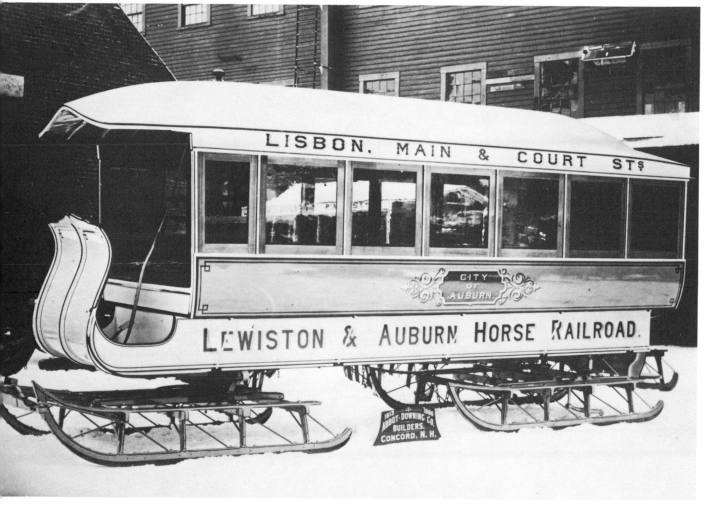

74. Peddler's sleigh. When snow fell, the local peddler could substitute this sleigh for his peddler's wagon. Just slightly larger than a regular cutter, and similar in design, it provides two rear compartments, another under the seat and a rail on top to retain small boxes or parcels. This was a most practical and serviceable arrangement for small merchandise. *The Hub,* vol. 37, July 1895, p. 263.

75. Stage sled. This vehicle provided one means of moving passengers in winter. The body, set on a pair of bobs, is basically that of a passenger wagon, but the construction of the dash and the driver's compartment indicates that the vehicle is not a conversion, but was built for use on runners. It had no

doors; curtains rolled down to cover the openings. They also cover the window openings, and the customary luggage rack is at the back. (Photograph from the Smithsonian Institution.)

76. Wagonette sled. In cities, omnibuses and wagonettes could be replaced in winter with rear-entrance sleds such as this one by the Abbot, Downing Co., of Concord, New Hampshire. A vehicle of the highest quality, with a brilliant finish, it is mounted on oscillating bobs, the rear one carrying a pair of spragging brakes that were operated by the long lever in the front. (Photograph courtesy the Concord Coach Society, Inc., Concord, New Hampshire.)

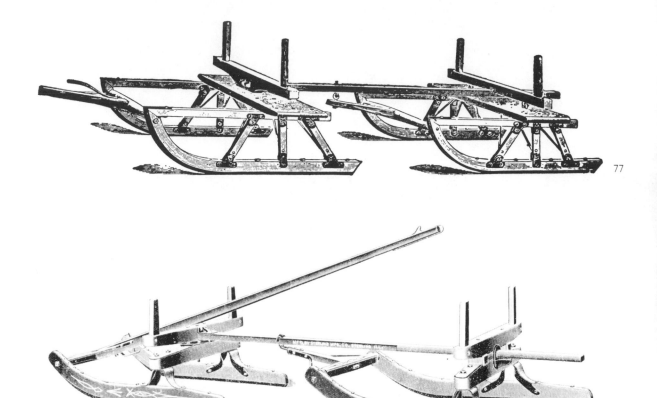

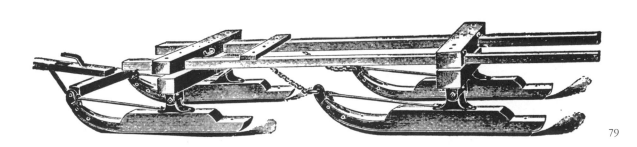

77. **Bobsled.** Practical for all sorts of winter transport, but especially used by farmers, this bobsled with three knees is typical. The body of a farm wagon was often transferred to this sled, but sometimes the runners carried a simple box 8″–10″ deep. A farm-wagon seat was frequently placed on the box. Cray Brothers, Cleveland, Ohio, catalog of 1910, p. 291.

78. **Bobsled.** Another design, of simplified construction, eliminated knees and raves by substituting pressed-steel fittings. The coupling pole of this sled passed through a revolving sleeve in the rear bob, facilitating movement of the vehicle over uneven ground by lending flexibility. Runner width of bobsleds was frequently 1¾″–2″. *The Farm Implement News,* Nov. 19, 1891, p. 14.

79. **Bobsled.** Here is a heavy sled used for purposes such as logging, a use for which no body was needed; the logs rested directly on the cross-members. Note the hinge joints between the runners and beams of this oscillating sled. Runners were

available in widths of 4″ and 5″. Cray Brothers, Cleveland, Ohio, catalog of 1910, p. 291.

80. **Coal wagon.** Heavy wagons that hauled coal needed to have some means of dumping, preferably into a chute, to deliver coal into a basement with minimal hand labor. This one has no dumping mechanism, but is built with a sloping floor. A small door at the rear controlled the discharge of the coal into the chute. Black body, striped with fine white lines. Vermilion gear, striped black. Wheels 37″ and 55″. *The Hub,* vol. 29, June 1887, pl. 25.

81. **Coal wagon.** Here is an efficient, hand-operated dumper that could be had in sizes up to five-ton capacity. Hinges at the front of the seat allowed it to be turned out of the way when the wagon was loaded. Chains under the body, attached to the lower ends of the eccentric arms, raise the body. Indian red body with black framework, striped red and white. Indian red gear, striped black and white. Warner wheels 38″ and 52″. *The Carriage Monthly,* vol. 36, Jan. 1901, pl. 386.

80

81

82. Coal wagon. This is the wagon of no. 81, shown in the dumping position. Turning the crank in the center of the wagon operates the gear train that winds up the chains which raise the body. Sheet-metal chutes were carried under the body. The small crank at the rear probably operates the small door through which the coal is discharged. *The Carriage Monthly,* vol. 37, Feb. 1902, pl. 556.

83. Coal wagon. Employing what is essentially the same mechanism used in no. 82, this is an elevating dump wagon, sometimes necessary when greater height was needed for dumping, as when dumping into a storage shed instead of a basement. Some elevating wagons raised the body to an even

greater height than this one. The chute is in its traveling position, under the body. *The Carriage Monthly,* vol. 44, Jan. 1909, pl. 1196.

84. Ice wagon. Neighborhood ice delivery required sturdy wagons, generally on platform springs, to carry the heavy loads of ice. Covered tops were preferred, but not essential, and an additional characteristic was the overhanging ends of the roof, which gave the ice even greater shelter from the sun's rays. Studebaker wagons were generally painted a cream color to reflect better the heat of the sun; the gear was red. Wheels 36" and 52". Studebaker Bros. Mfg. Co., South Bend, Indiana, catalog no. 223, 1903, p. 77.

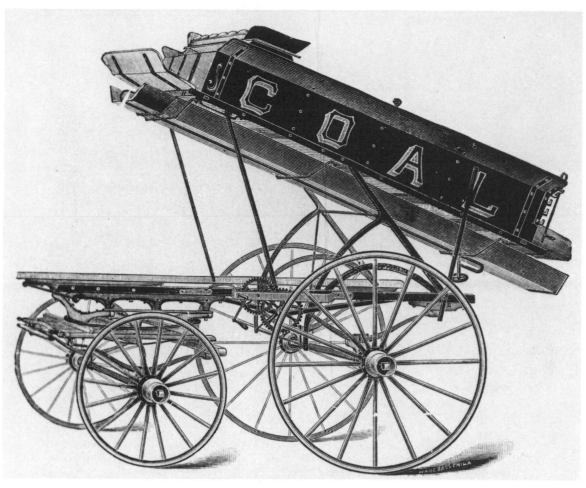

83

84

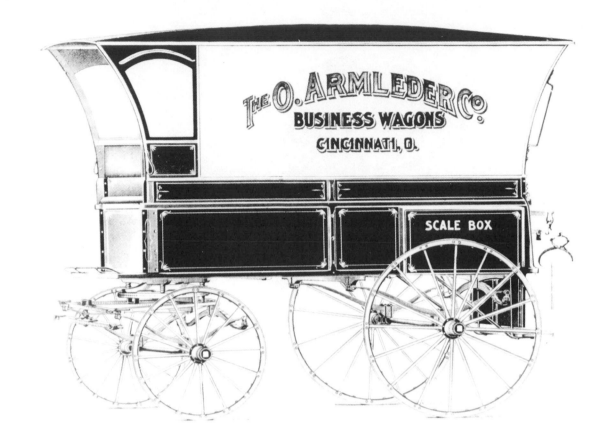

85

FINNESEY & KOBLER,
"THE MODEL SHOP."
Brown & 27th Sts.

86

85. Ice wagon. Some ice wagons were paneled to the roof, but many, like this one, were paneled for about two feet, the remainder being enclosed by painted cotton duck. Heavy slats protected the canvas on the inside. Characteristically, the wagons had large handles and a long step in the rear. The customary scale beam holds a balance scale. Wheels 34″ and 44″. The O. Armleder Co., Cincinnati, Ohio, catalog 34, ca. 1918, p. 53.

86. Ice wagon. A typical high-quality vehicle from the shops of Finnesey & Kobler, a well-known Philadelphia firm that specialized in fine commercial work. Ice wagons, built in one- and two-horse sizes, could haul from one to four tons. (Photograph from the Smithsonian Institution.)

87. Ice wagon. This model is not entirely typical, for it is a fairly ordinary medium-size delivery wagon. Like many ice wagons, it carries attractive and colorful paintings and scroll-work on the sides. Often the paintings portrayed polar scenes; this one reproduces Emanuel Leutze's famous depiction of George Washington crossing the ice-choked Delaware River. (Photograph from the Smithsonian Institution.)

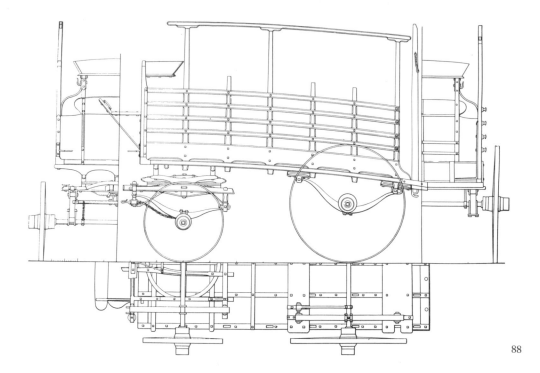

88

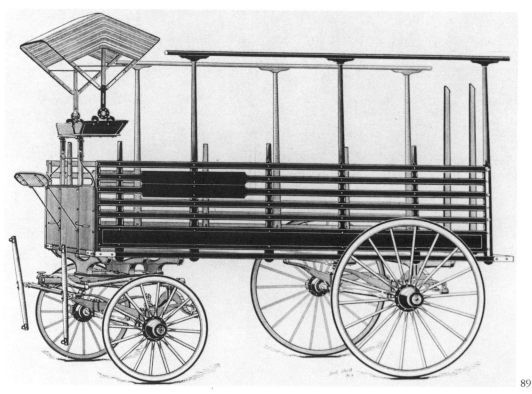

89

88. Truck. This type of truck was one of the more important freight movers in cities during the second half of the nineteenth century and the early years of the twentieth. The floor slopes downward in the rear for ease in loading, and rises in front so that the wheels can cut under the body, which gives a short turning radius for crowded city work. Suspension is usually on truck springs, which have the front end fixed, while the rear end slides. The rearmost stakes are also the loading skids. Wheels 34″ and 52″. *The Hub,* vol. 45, Jan. 1904, p. 377.

89. Truck. This larger two-horse truck shows an alternative method of suspension—platform springs. The driver's seat is protected by a sunshade, which could be adjusted to varying angles. Top rails were fitted to the long stakes to support a cloth cover. The end cut of the two rear stakes again indicated that they doubled as skids. Red body, striped black, with black chamfers. Red gear, striped black. Wheels 37″ and 55″. *The Hub,* vol. 43, Jan. 1902, pl. 545.

90

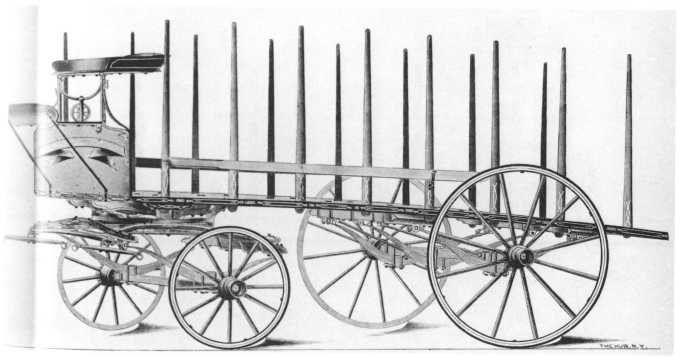

91

90. Truck. Another large two-horse truck features removable stakes at each side, so that both side- and end-loading were possible. The seat was often mounted on springs, as is this one, and most seats were hinged to turn over forward to be out of the way when loading. This four-ton truck cost $645. Dark green body with black chamfers and iron; striped gold. Yellow gear, striped red, or red, striped black. Cushion of brown duck. Wheels 36″ and 52″. Studebaker Bros. Mfg. Co., South Bend, Indiana, catalog no. 601, 1912, p. 99.

91. Truck. This is the common two-horse style, although a third truck spring in the center of the rear axle assists in supporting an extra-heavy load. The customary high driving seat enabled the driver to see and maneuver more precisely in crowded city streets. The loading skids are carried in brackets on the sides of the stakes. Red body and gear, striped black and fine-lined with white. Wheels 38″ and 56″. *The Hub*, vol. 26, Jan. 1885, pl. 82.

92

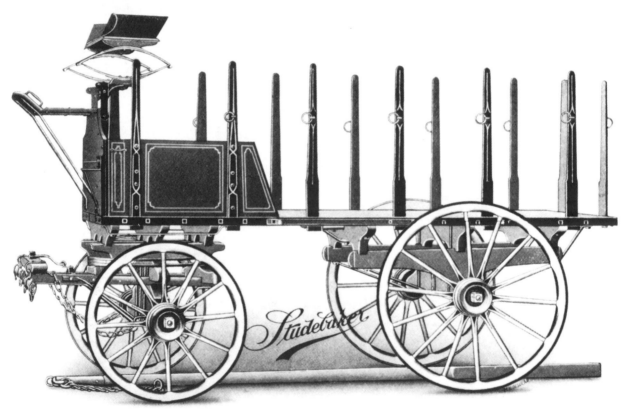

93

92. Truck. Suspension is provided by a combination of platform springs in front and truck springs in the rear. An unusual feature is the roller under the rear end of the floor. The truck floor was backed over a loading dock, the roller several inches above the dock. When the truck was loaded, the roller rested on the dock, and helped the vehicle to get free of the dock when the team moved away. Unlike most models, this truck has brakes. All vermilion, striped black and fine-lined with white. Wheels 38″ and 49″. *The Carriage Monthly*, vol. 16, May 1880, pl. 12.

93. Truck. Less common was the dead-axle truck without springs. The forward side panels as well as the stakes were removable. Wheels 38″ and 48″. Studebaker Bros. Mfg. Co., South Bend, Indiana, catalog no. 223, 1903, p. 72.

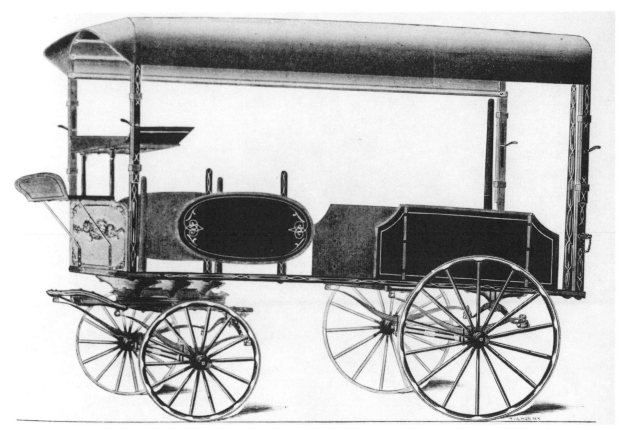

94

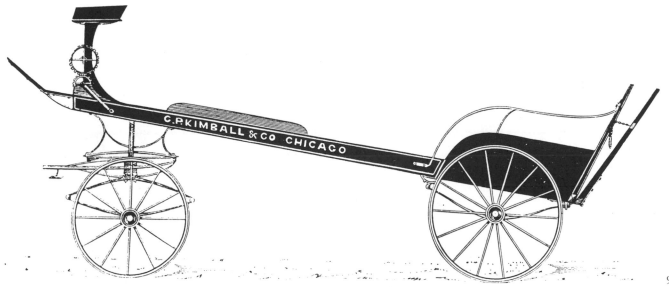

95

94. Furniture truck. Few trucks had canopy tops. This model had one as additional protection because the wagon carried furniture, and damage from a sudden shower could not be risked. Uncharacteristically, this top was made to move up and down to accommodate high pieces of furniture. All side panels were removable. Lake body. Vermilion gear, striped brown, edged with yellow. Wheels 37″ and 52″. *The Hub,* vol. 28, Oct. 1886, pl. 58.

95. Carriage-delivery truck. This truck was built by the famed Chicago builder, C. P. Kimball & Co., of the Maine family of carriage builders who developed the Portland cutter. The carriage, having been drawn up by the winch, was allowed to rest against the closed endgate, which also served as the loading ramp. One horse reportedly drew this, and could handle a 1600-pound landau with ease. Because of the nature of the loads, the rear track had to be unusually wide—86″ as opposed to the front track's 56″—to allow a standard-width carriage to pass between the rear wheels. Wheels 33″ and 38″. *The Hub,* vol. 23, July 1881, pl. 43.

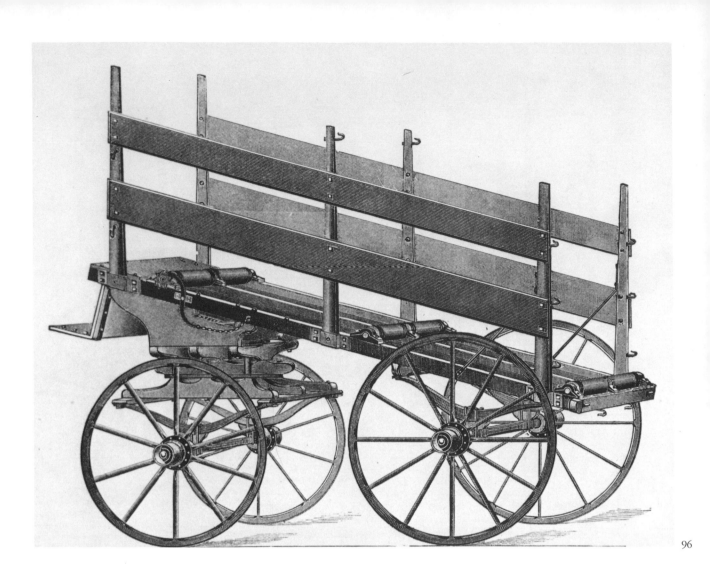

96

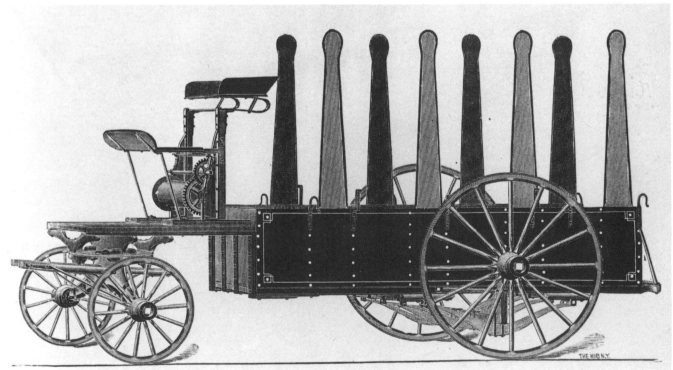

97

52

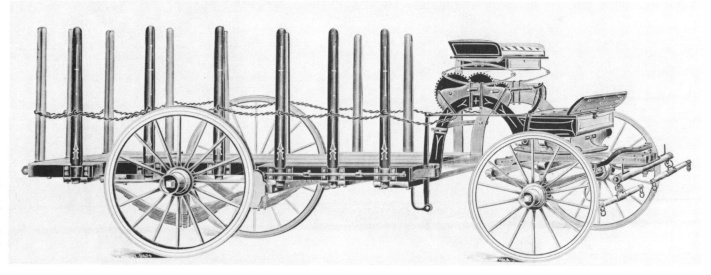

96. Lumber truck. Lumber was carefully stacked on this inclined floor, with all weight resting on the three rollers. To unload, the front roller was released, and the entire load rolled back, landing, it is to be hoped, as a unit on the ground. Vermilion body, striped black, fine-lined with white. Yellow gear, striped black, with a fine line of red. Wheels 43″ and 50″. *The Carriage Monthly,* vol. 17, Nov. 1881, pl. 69.

97. Glass truck. A special-purpose truck, this was made to deliver large sheets of plate glass. The front half of the gear is dead axle, but in the rear, four truck springs hang under the drop-center axle. A winch drew the glass onto the vehicle. Capacity was six tons. The entire vehicle was red, striped white and black. Wheels 34″ and 63″. *The Hub,* vol. 32, Aug. 1890, pl. 40.

98. Windlass truck. Equipped with a winch, like several of the special-purpose trucks, this general-purpose, seven-ton vehicle specialized in hauling anything that was unusually heavy or difficult to manage. The cranks could be attached to the upper shaft if great power were needed; to the middle shaft if less power was required. Dark green body with black moldings. English vermilion gear, striped black. Wheels 36″ and 48″ *The Hub,* vol. 26, Sept. 1884, pl. 49.

99. Crane-neck windlass truck. Similar in operation to the previous truck, except that it has a drop-center rear axle to lower the entire floor. Fore and aft, the floor extends slightly beyond the wheels. Built by the well-known Philadelphia firm of Fulton and Walker, the truck's capacity on good roads was about six tons. All carmine, striped white and black. Wheels 40″ and 48″. *The Carriage Monthly,* vol. 35, Dec. 1899, pl. 204.

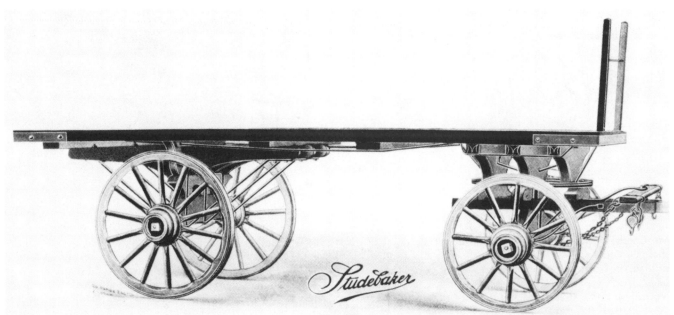

100. Crane-neck windlass truck. Another Philadelphia builder of commercial work constructed this truck on the same lines as no. 99. Tools, ropes and chains could be carried in the box under the footboards. (Photograph from the Smithsonian Institution.)

101. Dray. The dray was similar to the truck, and was often confused with it, even by the builders, who sometimes used the terms synonymously. The dray usually had rear wheels smaller than the truck's, their tops being lower than the floor, so that a load could extend out over the wheels. Front wheels almost always cut under for sharp turning, and the dray most often had no springs. This one cost $240. Wheels 36″ and 40″. Studebaker Bros. Mfg. Co., South Bend, Indiana, catalog no. 223, 1903, p. 71.

102

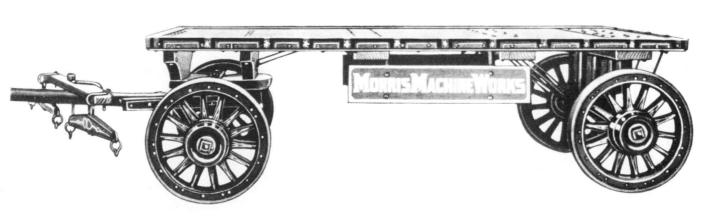

103

102. Dray. Although heavy movers frequently had no driving seat, this one has a seat similar to that of a truck. The iron stakes could be put into any of the many holes in the floor to help secure the load. Used for some of the heaviest work, drays were a favorite of industry, whereas the truck was a favorite of business. Owensboro Wagon Co., Owensboro, Kentucky, catalog no. 8 of ca. 1913, p. 66.

103. Dray. A particularly heavy dray, of ten-ton capacity, this was intended for carrying heavy machinery and castings that needed to be machined. There were no protrusions to get in the way of loading. The Haywood Wagon Co., Newark, New York, catalog of ca. 1910, p. 30.

104

105

104. Dray. Not all drays were heavy. This is a one-horse size with only 2500-pound capacity. The driver could walk, stand on the floor, or perhaps sit on a part of the load. Black or Brewster green body on a red running gear. Wheels 32″ and 36″. Piedmont Wagon & Mfg. Co., Hickory, North Carolina, catalog of ca. 1910, p. 36.

105. Crane-neck dray. This special-purpose low-hung dray was used by the Pullman Company shops, at Pullman, Illinois, in 1903, to carry parts of railway cars. Most drays did not have brakes, which left the entire responsibility for braking with the horses. (Photograph from the Smithsonian Institution.)

106. Express wagon. An important mover of city freight was the express or baggage wagon. Closely associated with railway shipping, they were extensively used for express-company deliveries, railway-baggage movement and large deliveries from business houses. Characteristically, they were on platform springs, had flareboards and a high driving seat. This typical express wagon has an extra helper spring in the rear. A two-ton wagon was priced at $420; a three-ton cost $490. Red body with black chamfers and irons, striped gold. Yellow gear, striped red. Brown duck cushion. Wheels 36″ and 48″. Studebaker Bros. Mfg. Co., South Bend, Indiana, catalog no. 601, 1912, p. 95.

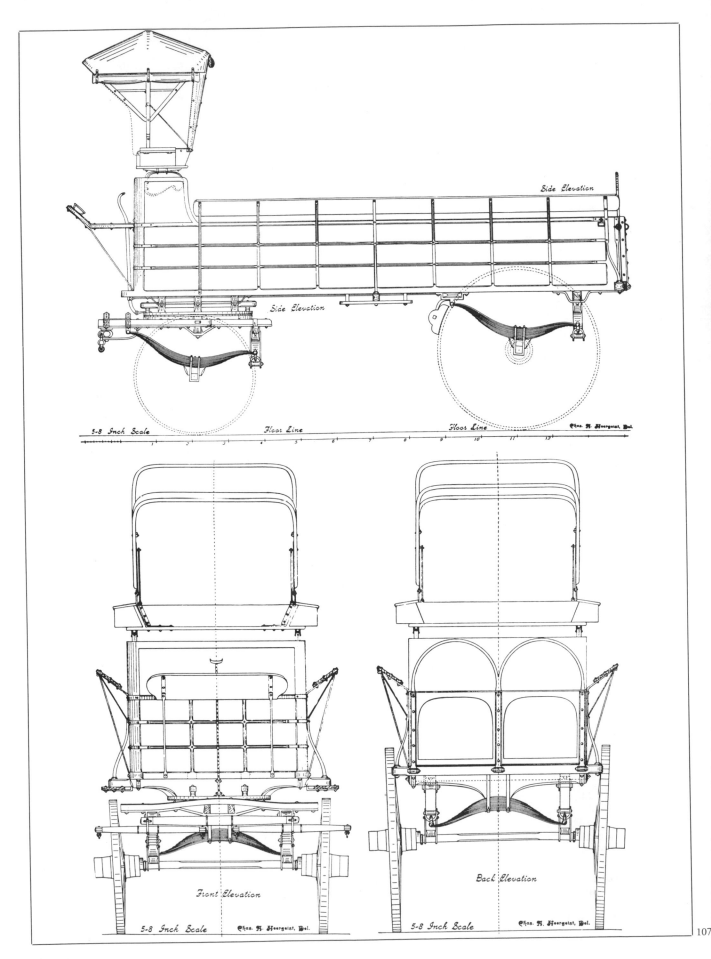

Side Elevation

Side Elevation

5-8 Inch Scale   Floor Line   Floor Line   Chas. R. Hoergelat, Del.

Front Elevation

Back Elevation

5-8 Inch Scale   Chas. R. Hoergelat, Del.

5-8 Inch Scale   Chas. R. Hoergelat, Del.

107

108

109

107. Express wagon. A fine example of a high-quality wagon, this shows paneled sides, rounded corners and a storm top with both rear and side curtains. These vehicles, including this model, were more likely than trucks or drays to have brakes. A box for tools, papers, ropes, etc., is fitted to each side of the seat. *The Carriage Monthly,* vol. 42, Jan. 1907, pp. 268–269.

108. Express wagon. Another version had a canopy top, like this one, operated by the Adams Express Company. The manner in which the top is attached made flareboards less practical, so they were omitted. Chrome green body with black

moldings and fine lines of yellow. Vermilion gear, striped yellow. Wheels 38½″ and 52″. *The Carriage Monthly,* vol. 16, Dec. 1880, pl. 71.

109. Express wagon. A lighter-weight express wagon with the driving seat lowered, this was equipped with a whiffletree and a pole socket, so that one or two horses could be used. For greater security of the load, heavy screen sides were fitted, giving these vehicles the name "screen wagons." Many had doors fitted above the endgate. Wheels 36″ and 48″. *The Carriage Monthly,* vol. 49, June 1913, p. 32.

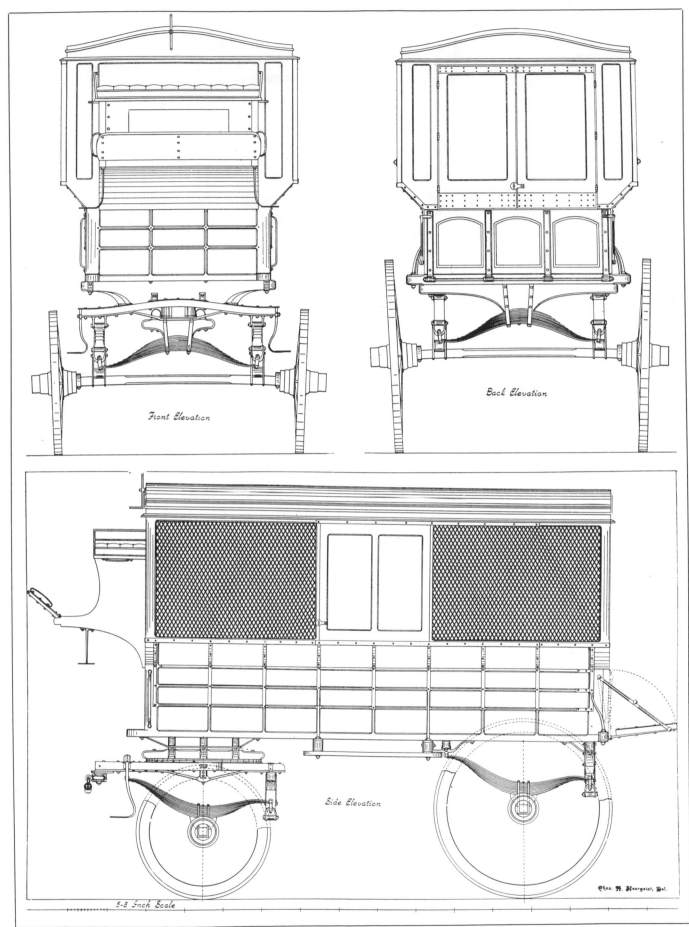

Front Elevation

Back Elevation

Side Elevation

5-8 Inch Scale

Chas. H. Heergeist, Del.

of them must remain on seat, unless the loading or unloading of wagon requires the services of both men.

26 Wagonmen will constantly keep as **tight a rein as the horses will bear,** thus **maintaining proper control** of them in starting, trotting, walking or stopping.

27 Whipping, jerking or abusing horses in any way **is forbidden,** and if done, will subject the employe at fault to immediate discharge. **The Company does not want, nor will it have, any man in charge of horses who is brutal or unkind in his treatment of them.**

28 Fast driving is strictly forbidden, except when absolutely necessary to connect with trains or boats.

29 In driving around **corners** or **over street crossings** or **railway tracks,** horses should **not be driven faster than a walk,** and must be held **under perfect control. Tracks** should be **crossed at right angles.** Before turning corners, wagonmen **must signal with the hand or whip** when the turn is to be made and in what direction. **In turning corners,** wagons going to the **right** should be kept to the **right of the center** of the street and as near the right-hand curb as possible, and vehicles turning to the **left** should be kept to the **right of the center of the two intersecting streets,** before turning.

30 Wagons must not be **stopped suddenly,** nor **started to turn,** without first warning those behind by signal with hand or whip or otherwise.

31 Wagonmen must **not** drive or back their wagons **upon the sidewalks** of city streets.

10

32 Before turning out or starting from or stopping at the **curb line,** wagonman must see that there is **sufficient space** free from other vehicles so that such turn, start or stop may be **safely made,** and then give a plainly visible or audible signal.

33 In driving in streets where there are **car tracks,** wagons **must not be driven on the track** when there is room for them elsewhere.

34 To avoid **damage** or **injury** to horses, wagons or other property, whether of this Company or others, wagonmen will **always take the safe course** by **avoiding all possible chances of collision,** even though they may have to sacrifice their "rights to the road."

35 Wagons must be driven on the **right** side of the street. In **meeting vehicles coming from opposite** direction **pass to the right.** Other vehicles **going in the same direction** must be passed on the **left side.**

36 Wagonmen must **not** rein horses either to the right or to the left **without first looking behind on the side of the wagon they are to turn,** to see that no one is approaching or in the way.

37 Surface cars in cities usually have the **right of way** along their tracks between cross streets over all other vehicles moving in the same direction at a less rate of speed, and wagonmen must turn out as soon as possible upon signal by the car driver or motorman.

38 **Right of way of certain vehicles.** The officers and men of the Fire Department and Fire Patrol, (where they exist) with their fire apparatus of all kinds, when going to, or on duty at, or returning from a fire, and all Ambulances, and the officers and men and vehicles of the Police De-

11

110. Express wagon. A more unusual design of express wagon had more complete security provided by a paneled front, screen sides and rear doors. The driving seat, more like that of a stagecoach, is also uncommon. A step on both sides assisted a helper in passing packages through the side doors. Wheels 40″ and 54″. *The Carriage Monthly,* vol. 37, Feb. 1902, pp. 408 and 411.

111. Express wagon. A pair of Baltimore & Ohio Railroad wagons stand ready to roll. Most city vehicles used one or two horses, but more could be used if necessary, as seen here. This photograph was taken ca. 1900 at the B&O's Mt. Clare Shops in Baltimore. (Photograph from the Smithsonian Institution.)

112. Expressmen's instructions. A sampling from the *Instructions to Wagonmen,* issued to drivers by the American Express Company in 1905. (Manual from the Smithsonian Institution.)

when Children are in the Streets, or when Ladies
or Children are about to cross the Streets, as they
~~are~~ frequently uncertain and confused in their movements.
**TEAMS SHOULD BE BROUGHT TO A FULL STOP,
UNTIL ALL UNCERTAINTY IS REMOVED.**

113. Expressmen's warning sign. This sign was once posted by the American Express Company at a point at which their drivers were about to depart from company property. It is not likely to meet the approval of today's women's liberation groups. (Smithsonian Institution.)

114. Express wagon. In April 1904, the Automobile Club of America conducted a competition between horse and motor vehicles in New York City. One of the horses of the middle wagon quizzically studies the 1904 Moyea truck, which is fitted with an express-type body. (Photograph in the Smithsonian Institution.)

115. Stage wagon. The first public stages in America were nothing more than primitive covered wagons, with several unpadded, backless benches running across the body. Neither springs nor thoroughbraces were employed to ease the ride. This illustration, from an advertisement in *The Pennsylvania Gazette* of April 24, 1760, gives some idea of the style.

116. Stage wagon. Shortly after the covered wagon-stage came a vehicle that began to borrow the lines of a coach. It lacked doors, the only entrance being through the open front. Most of the passengers sat on the four benches, another one or two rode on the front seat with the driver. Ladies were given the rear seat, as it was the only one with a backrest. Suspension was on thoroughbraces carried by iron jacks. Curtains could be rolled down over the side openings in foul weather. Illustration by J. Weld, 1800.

115

117. Stage wagon. A detail from a broadside dated 1821, just about the earliest date for this type, showing the next step in stage development. Now we see a luggage rack, a door in the side and the front passenger seat facing the rear, while the driver is outside. (Smithsonian Institution.)

118. Stagecoach. By the 1820s, possibly slightly earlier, the true coach design was coming into use in public vehicles. Here is a drawing which Capt. Basil Hall produced with the aid of a camera lucida in about 1827–28. The immediate forerunner of the Troy and Concord types, this coach lacks the flat roof that

made possible the top luggage railing and the additional roof seat. (From *Travels in North America in 1827–1828,* by Capt. Basil Hall.)

119. Concord coach. In 1827, J. Stephens Abbot, then in the employ of Lewis Downing, of Concord, New Hampshire, built the first coach of this type. While he is generally given full credit for the design, evidence indicates that the Troy coaches (those built in the area of Troy, New York), by Veazie, Eaton, and Gould, and possibly others, were actually earlier and almost identical in detail. This hotel coach, seating six

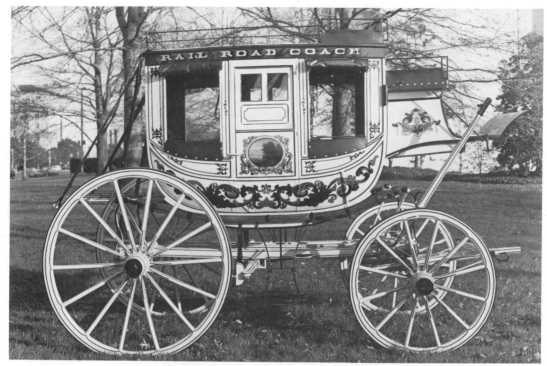

119

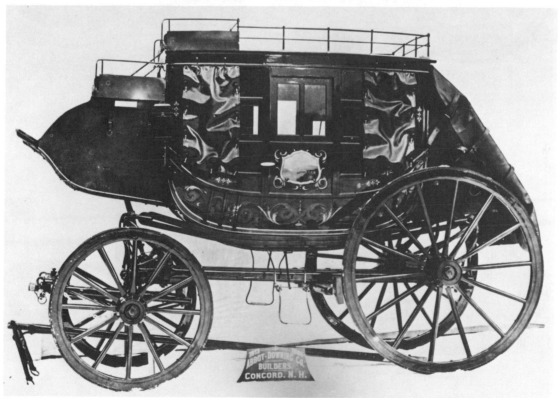

120

passengers inside, is one of the earliest known survivors, having been built in 1848 in the shops of Lewis Downing, following the 1847 split of the Abbot and Downing partnership. Straw-color body and gear, striped black and ornately decorated with red, green and brown scrollwork, oil paintings and gold leaf. (Coach in the Smithsonian Institution.)

120. Concord coach. Here is a typical Abbot, Downing stage that seated nine passengers (three each on three inside seats, including the jump seat) and carried four or five more passengers alongside and behind the driver. This was the size commonly used for road travel between cities and towns. A large quantity of luggage could be carried on the roof, in the boot under the driver's seat and on the leather-covered rack in the rear. Most stage lines also had contracts to carry the mails and many offered parcel-express service as well. The leather thoroughbrace suspension can be seen under the body of this coach, which in the 1880s was priced at $1100. (Photograph from the Meade Simpson collection.)

65

121

122

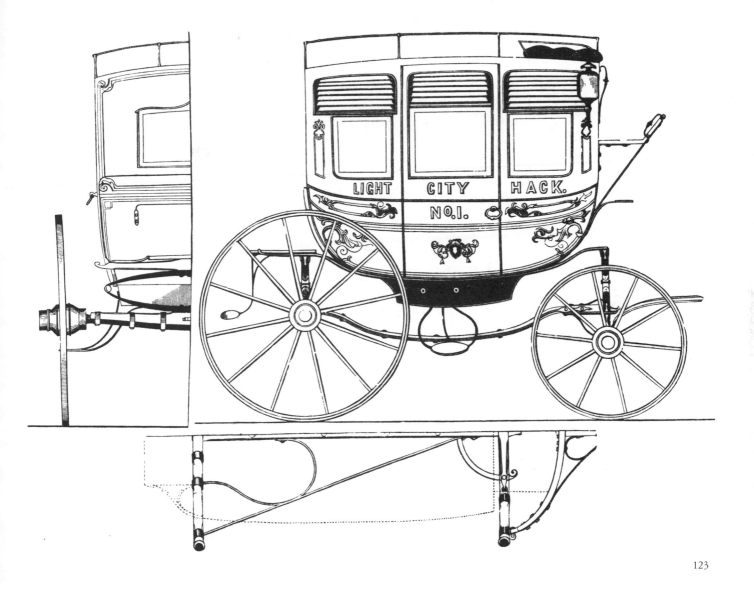

123

121. **Concord coach.** One of the largest built, this coach probably carried 12 passengers inside on two regular seats and two rows of jump seats. Additional passengers rode on the roof seats and alongside the driver. (A few coaches were also built to accommodate 16 passengers inside.) Some of these large coaches were road coaches and carried mail, but many others were used by resort hotels as excursion and outing vehicles. In addition to the scrollwork, the coaches had colorful paintings on the doors, surrounded by gold leaf. This coach probably had the customary red body on a straw-color gear. (Photograph from the Meade Simpson collection.)

122. **Stagecoach.** This elegant eight-horse coach, combining the body lines of a Concord with the front and rear boots of an English road coach, was built by the New York Transfer Co., in New York City. While it has the roof seats of an excursion coach, this one actually was put into public service. It seated 23 outside, who used the inside during storms. It had French windows, closed by wooden shutters. Red body panels; blue moldings; blue boots; the front and rear panels and the front seat risers of red; panels ornately decorated with scrolls and paintings. White gear, striped with a broad line of red and two fine lines of blue. Wheels 44″ and 63″. *The Hub,* vol. 19, 1878, pl. 94. (Collection of the Library of Congress.)

123. **City stage.** While the sign on this six-passenger stage indicates it was a cab, its comparatively greater capacity suggests it was used as a hotel coach. It may have been owned by a private operator who carried passengers from depots to hotels that were too small to own their own coaches. Unlike a Concord, the driver sits on a roof seat. The rear platform could carry a footman or be of use in placing luggage on the roof. Wheels 34″ and 46″. *The American Coachmakers' Magazine,* vol. 3, Feb. 1857, pl. 5.

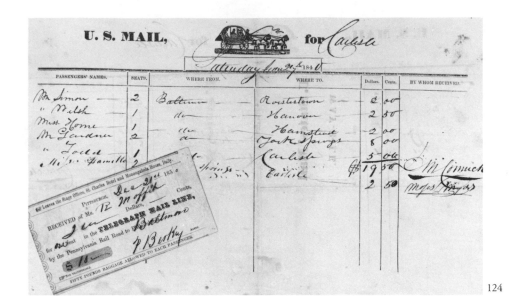

124

125

124. Waybill and ticket. Drivers of mail stages carried waybills that recorded passengers, destinations, fares, etc. The cut at the top, while it may have been obsolete in 1840, when this trip was made, may also indicate a rather long transitional period from the oval coach to the Troy/Concord types. The ticket shows that travel was not inexpensive. (Originals in the Smithsonian Institution.)

125. Road coach. This vehicle, built by Brewster & Co., New York City, was patterned after the English road coach. Although some of the wealthy men who owned them used

them for travel and for sport driving, some operated them as public coaches, for they felt it more challenging to maintain close schedules than simply to drive for amusement. Luggage went on top and in the rear boot. (From *A Manual of Coaching,* by Fairman Rogers, New York, 1899.)

126. Passenger wagons. An Abbot, Downing advertising sheet presents a number of less-expensive wagons that were designed for use as public stages. All were on thoroughbrace suspension. (From the Smithsonian Institution.)

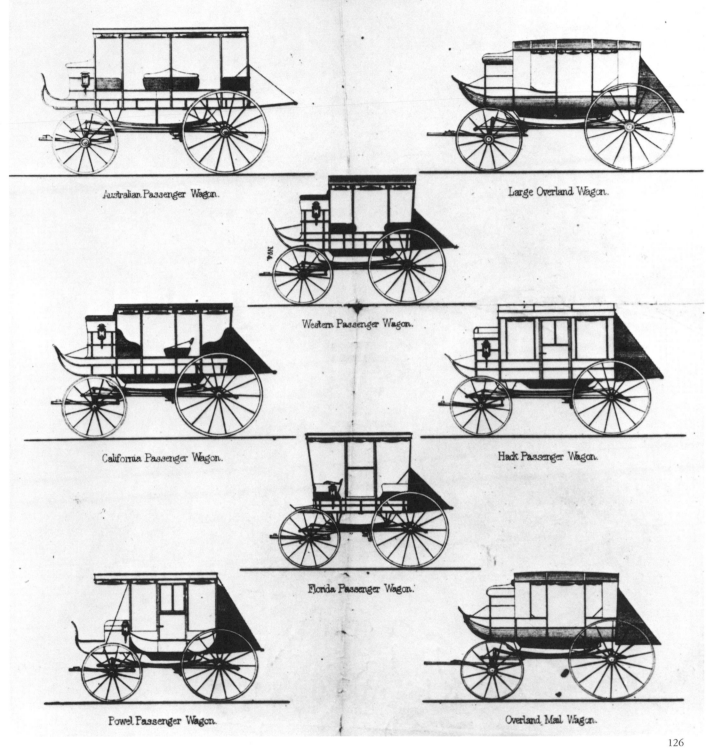

ABBOT, DOWNING & CO.

CONCORD, N.H. U.S.A.

Australian Passenger Wagon.

Large Overland Wagon.

Western Passenger Wagon.

California Passenger Wagon.

Hack Passenger Wagon.

Florida Passenger Wagon.

Powel Passenger Wagon.

Overland Mail Wagon.

126

69

127

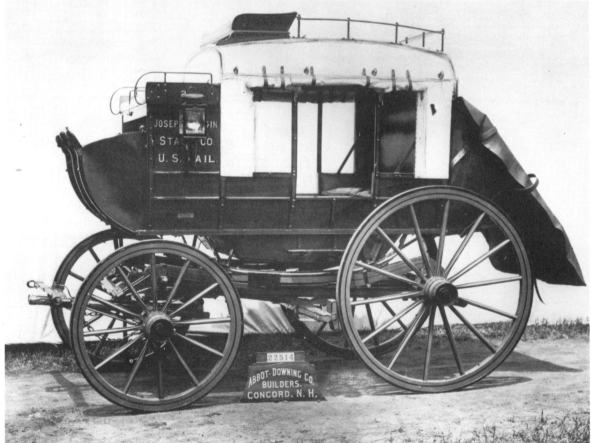

128

129

127. Hack passenger wagon. Priced around $600, about half the price of a Concord coach, this provided essentially the same comfort. Since it was used on the poorer roads, and was consequently often bespattered with mud, it was sometimes called a mud wagon. Usually made in six- and nine-passenger sizes, these wagons could carry a large amount of baggage, mail and express packages in the front boot, on the top and on the rear luggage rack. (Photograph from the Meade Simpson collection.)

128. Overland wagon. An even more primitive passenger wagon, this enjoyed great popularity in the West. The adjusting turnbuckle can be seen joining the ends of the thoroughbrace on its underside. Passengers found it precarious to mount and alight from these vehicles. (Photograph from the Meade Simpson collection.)

129. Passenger wagon. Here is a serviceable stage by M. P. Henderson & Son, a prominent California firm that specialized in such work. The builder used much heavier brake shoes, which were often required for mountainous Western travel. (Photograph from the Meade Simpson collection.)

130

131

130. Yellowstone wagon. Both Henderson and the Abbot, Downing Co. built these vehicles for the federal government. Constructed on a thoroughbrace carriage like that of the passenger wagon, they were used to convey tourists in Western parks. Rear luggage accommodation was small. Sometimes the wagons were fitted with a canopy top. (Photograph from the Meade Simpson collection.)

131. Mountain wagon. Among the simplest of stages were these mountain wagons, which were nothing more than extra-long spring wagons with three or four seats under a canopy top and a luggage rack. Rarely used for long trips, they were popular for such work as carrying passengers from rail-depot towns to towns nearby. Dark green body on a red or yellow gear, striped black. Wheels 42″ and 48″. Studebaker Bros. Mfg. Co., South Bend, Indiana, catalog no. 224, 1904, p. 108.

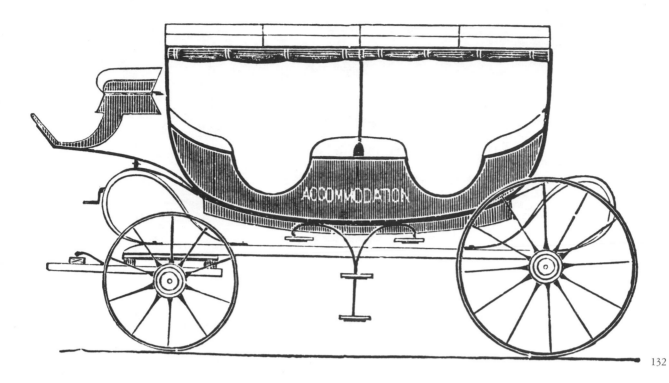

132

133

132. Accommodation. Built by Wade and Leverich of New York City for Abraham Brower, this was the first American carriage for public service in cities. It was put in operation ca. 1827 for regular service on Broadway between Bleecker and Wall Streets. Suspended on thoroughbraces, it carried 12 passengers. (From *The World on Wheels,* 1878, by Ezra Stratton, p. 432.)

133. Sociable. Following his success with the accommodation coach, Brower had the same builders construct this vehicle in 1829, and used it as a companion piece to the accommodation. Still on thoroughbraces, it was a rear-entrance vehicle, and had seats running along the length of both sides, marking it as the immediate predecessor of the omnibus. (From *The World on Wheels,* 1878, by Ezra Stratton, p. 432.)

134

135

134. Omnibus. In 1831 Brower had this vehicle built by John Stephenson of New York City, who appears to have borrowed some of the design of Wade and Leverich's sociable. This first American omnibus had four elliptic springs, above which the body was suspended on four leather braces. When this suspension proved unsatisfactory, Stephenson substituted platform springs, which also eliminated the perch connecting the front and rear gearing. A boy stood on the rear platform to collect the fare. (From *The World on Wheels,* 1878, by Ezra Stratton, p. 438.)

135. Omnibus. Soon the fore and aft sections of Stephenson's buses were eliminated, and the center panel was extended the entire length of the vehicle. The driving seat was then placed on the roof. Following these alterations, the design of the omnibus saw virtually no change to the end of the horse-drawn era. The bus shown here, though built for one of Stephenson's New Zealand customers, is entirely typical of the type. Built in varying lengths, this more common size carried 12 to 14 seated passengers, plus standees. Stephenson became the nation's foremost omnibus builder. (Photograph from the Smithsonian Institution.)

136

137

136. Omnibus. This Stephenson model of 1875 was probably the largest omnibus ever built. It was reportedly drawn by ten horses and carried 120 passengers, but it is hard to imagine handling a ten-horse team in a crowded city, and it also seems unlikely that it could hold that many passengers, even with standees. The powerful screw-operated brakes acted on both sides of the rear wheels. It would be interesting to know the final disposition of this bus. In 1914 George Schlitz of Brooklyn, New York, motorized it by attaching a Knox-Martin tractor and operated it as a picnic-excursion bus. Schlitz intended to send it from New York to the Panama-Pacific Exposition in San Francisco, via the Lincoln Highway. (Photograph from the Smithsonian Institution.)

137. Double-deck omnibus. These vehicles were not nearly as popular in the United States as they were in London, but they were used in a few of the larger cities such as New York and Philadelphia. This omnibus, by the prominent Philadelphia firm of Fulton and Walker, ran on that city's Broad Street, and carried the so-called knife-board seats on top. Some used garden seats, which faced forward. Main panels, lemon yellow; black moldings and concave panels; corner pillars red between moldings; area around windows, white; yellow top rail; white letter board with black letters shaded red. Morocco leather trimmings. Wheels 44″ and 56″. *The Carriage Monthly,* vol. 26, Sept. 1890, pl. 41.

138

139

138. Wagonette. A less expensive omnibus was suitable for service during the summer. Featuring the same seating arrangement as the omnibus, the wagonette is an open vehicle with a canopy top that extended over the driving seat. Curtains protected passengers in inclement weather. The Studebaker wagonette shown here was available in an eight-passenger size for $560, 12-passenger for $595 and 16-passenger for $640. Dark green body, striped carmine. Dark green gear, striped carmine, or carmine, striped black. Leather trimmed. Wheels 36″ and 46″. Studebaker Bros. Mfg. Co., South Bend, Indiana, catalog no. 224, 1903, p. 85.

139. Wagonette-omnibus. The omnibus body with the lowered seat of the wagonette caused many builders to call this a wagonette-omnibus, yet others called it an omnibus because it had glass windows. This ten-passenger model had glass frames that could be removed for summer use. *The Carriage Monthly,* vol. 34, Feb. 1899, pl. 66.

140

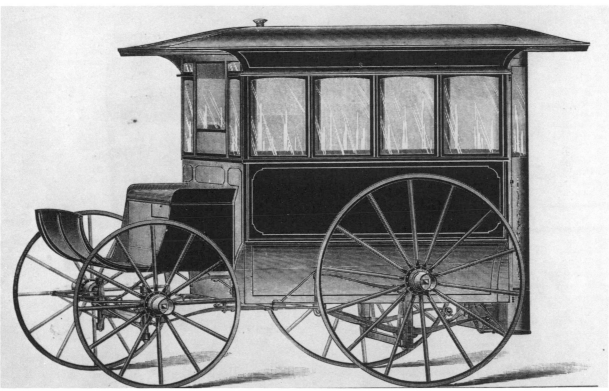

141

140. Wagonette-omnibus. This fine example was used by the Baltimore & Ohio Railroad to transfer passengers between Baltimore's two railway stations. Many such vehicles were owned by hotels, which used them like hotel coaches between hotels and depots. By the end of the nineteenth century, as it came to be considered more practical for the purpose, the wagonette had nearly supplanted the hotel coach. (Photograph from the Smithsonian Institution.)

141. Herdic. An interesting variant in this class of vehicles (named after its inventor, Peter Herdic) has features allowing easier access: a drop-center rear axle to lower the body, and a full-length door with the step inside. Another notable feature is the fixed front axle, equipped with steering knuckles, similar to automotive-type steering. Body, Tuscan red below glass frames and black above; natural-finish glass frames. Yellow gear, striped black. Red plush trimmings. Wheels 48″ and 60″. *The Carriage Monthly,* vol. 17, Apr. 1881, pl. 2.

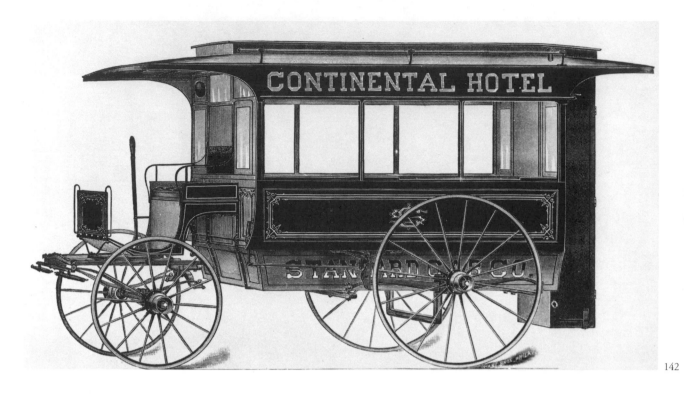

142

143

142. Wagonette-omnibus. A Fulton and Walker vehicle with conventional steering, this uses the drop-center rear axle and the full-length door of the Herdic for easier access. Tuscan red main panels; black upper and lower panels, front seat and back end. Enamel leather trimmings. Wheels 41″ and 55½″. *The Carriage Monthly,* vol. 23, Nov. 1887, pl. 71.

143. Hotel wagonette. Although this carriage appears to be an elongated depot wagon with its side doors, it is a wagonette because of the seating arrangement. In the rear are two longitudinal seats for two passengers each, and a folding seat across the front that carries two more. The carriage was used in the same manner as a hotel coach. Black body trimmed with dark green cloth. Yellow gear, striped black. Wheels 42″ and 49″. *The Carriage Monthly,* vol. 26, May 1890, pl. 16.

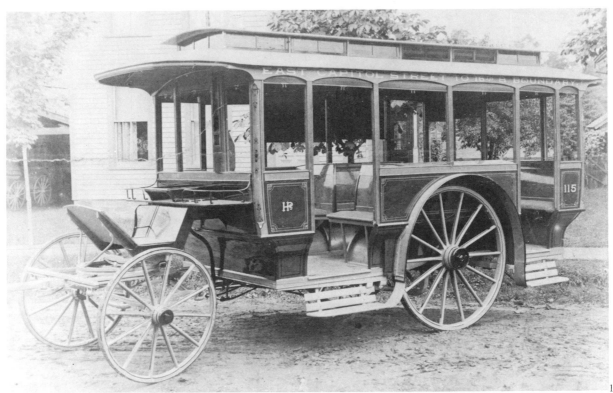

144

145

144. Herdic phaeton. This may be an incorrect name for such an oddity, operated in Washington, D.C., by the Herdic Phaeton Company, the initials of which appear on the front panel. A cross between a wagonette and a summer streetcar, it is but a token indication of the many variants in use during the late nineteenth century. (Photograph from the Robert H. Renneberger collection.)

145. Horsecar. Prior to the electrification of street railways, cars such as this one by the John Stephenson Co. were drawn over the rails by one or two horses. This smaller rear-entrance, one-horse car operated in Baltimore, Maryland, about 1890. There were no shafts for the animal, and consequently the harness had no breeching, so that the car employed mechanical brakes that were operated by the crank at the front. The sloping chute seen inside the car carried the fares to the fare box at the front, eliminating the need for a fare boy at the rear. (Photograph from the Smithsonian Institution.)

146

147

146. Horsecar. For summer use, open side-entrance cars like this Stephenson-built example were popular. If the weather turned bad, the striped curtains could be let down. This car operated between two communities in western Massachusetts in the mid-1880s. Some convertible cars had side panels and windows that could be removed for summer use. (Photograph from the Smithsonian Institution.)

147. New York cab. Early vehicles used for hire were usually various second-hand carriages. Many had serious shortcomings, such as being too heavy or cumbersome, so more efficient designs were sought. Compactness and maneuverability, desirable qualities, are displayed by this rear-entrance New York cab, which resembles a small omnibus and offers the same seating arrangement. *The Hub,* vol. 13, 1871, p. 30.

148. **Herdic cab.** Borrowing the drop-center axle and full-length door of the four-wheel, omnibus-type Herdic, this two-wheel version served as a public cab. Two-wheel cabs were popular because of their compactness and high maneuverability, but they offered a less pleasant ride than did four-wheelers, since the movements of the horse could be felt. Wheels 60″. *The Carriage Monthly,* vol. 17, May 1881, pl. 10.

149. **Gurney cab.** Patented by J. T. Gurney of Boston, this cab featured a body covered largely with sheet iron. Entered through a rear door, the cab had an omnibus-type seating arrangement for four passengers. Black upper panels; olive lower panels; white canework; striped gold and carmine. Black gear, striped orange glazed with carmine. Maroon plush trimming. Wheels 52″. *The Hub,* vol. 25, Feb. 1884, pl. 94.

150

THE HUB N.Y.

151

82

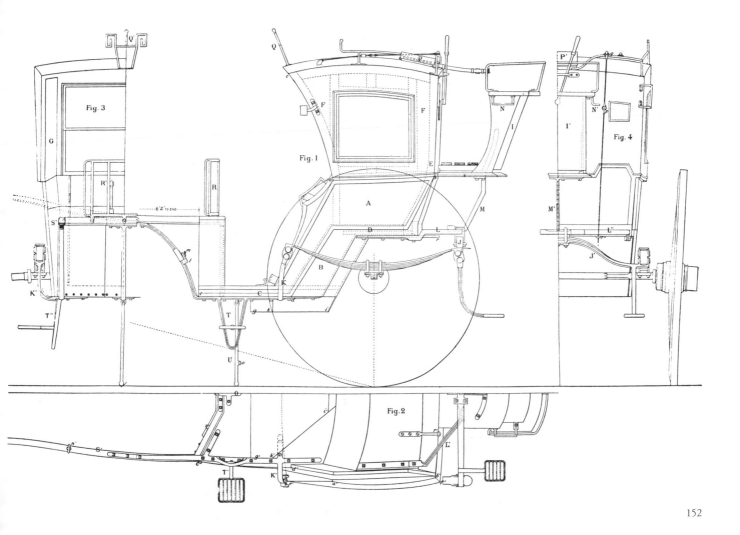

150. Extension-front brougham. This carriage, and its near relatives the clarence and the coupé, were originally intended as private carriages, but all were also popular as public cabs. The number on the lamp of the carriage seems to indicate that it was a public vehicle. It could be fitted for use with either one or two horses. Access was easy because of the relatively low suspension of the body. (Photograph from the Smithsonian Institution.)

151. Sedan cab. This unusual two-wheeler, built and patented by Chauncey Thomas of Boston, featured a rear entrance. Opening the door raised the divided seat and closing it lowered the seat, putting the passengers in a forward-facing position. The crank at the driver's right moved the body forward or backward to balance the load better according to weight, or for ascending or descending hills. Dark blue lower quarters and

door panels; black upper panels and moldings, striped Naples yellow. Dark blue gear, striped Naples yellow. Wheels 54". *The Hub,* vol. 26, Jan. 1885, pl. 78.

152. Hansom cab. This vehicle, developed in England between 1834 and 1873, was not successfully introduced into the United States until later in the century, when it enjoyed moderate popularity in several large cities, especially in New York. The introduction of rubber tires in the early 1890s noticeably improved a mediocre ride, helping to make the Hansom more acceptable. From his seat in the rear, the driver could open the double doors with a lever, and raise the window sash with a strap. The device on the front of the roof supported the driving lines. Wheels 57". *The Hub,* vol. 40, Aug. 1898, p. 332.

Prang & Mayer's Lith. Boston.

153

A.H.Markley - Phil.

154

153. Fire engine. Although the early hand-pumped fire engines were man-drawn (as were some later steam pumpers), the heavier steam engines were drawn by horses. This 1860 engine, built by the Amoskeag Mfg. Co., of Manchester, New Hampshire, featured two double-acting pumps that were operated by twin vertical cylinders. Weighing 7000 pounds empty, it could throw one stream of water 275 feet, or four streams simultaneously 160 feet. The 36″-diameter boiler carried three hundred 1¼″ × 24″ tubes. Wheels 54″ and 60″. Amoskeag leaflet, 1860.

154. Fire engine. The later engines often had this crane-neck frame, allowing sharper turning of the wheels. The rigid hose on the side brackets, with the strainer at the end, is the suction hose, and was put into a pond or stream to supply water. Usually drawn by two horses, the heavier engines could also be drawn by three horses abreast, to keep the unit compact for cramped city use. Five sizes of this 1899 Amoskeag weighed from 5600 to 9000 pounds and pumped from 500 to 1100 gallons per minute. Manchester Locomotive Works, Manchester, New Hampshire, catalog of 1899, p. 13.

155

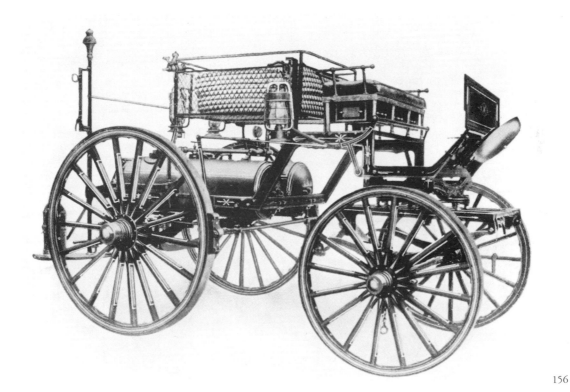

156

155. Fire engine. Similar in appearance to no. 154, but employing a different type of engine and pump, is this 1902 engine of The LaFrance Fire Engine Co., of Elmira, New York. Both the engine and the pump are of the rotary type. The box at the rear of the firebox and boiler carried coal, but the larger supply needed to maintain the fire had to be brought in another vehicle. LaFrance Fire Engine Co. catalog of 1902, p. 33.

156. Chemical engine. This twin-tank engine extinguished fires with carbonic acid, made by mixing sulphuric acid and bicarbonate of soda. Acid was carried in lead jars attached to the agitator shafts in 55-gallon tanks. The operator released the acid and turned the crank on the agitator shaft to mix the solution. The hose is in the top basket. Nott Fire Engine Co., Minneapolis, Minnesota, catalog of 1907.

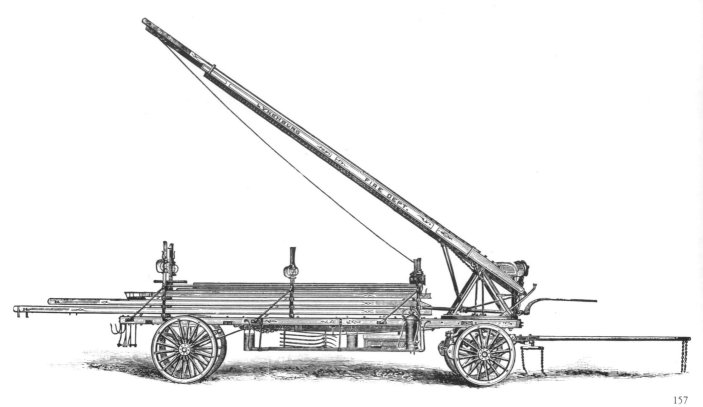

157

158

157. Ladder wagon. The LaFrance Engine Co. offered this Hayes extension-ladder truck in sizes from 45′ to 85′. A hand-operated screw elevates the ladder, and a drum and cable extend it to full height, the entire operation requiring only 40 seconds. In addition, one ground extension ladder and six single ladders are carried underneath, as well as shovels, axes, hooks, poles, fire extinguishers and other equipment. LaFrance Engine Co. catalog of 1902, p. 51.

158. Hose wagon. Similar in style to a delivery wagon, this vehicle carried folded hoses in the body, and nozzles and wrenches in the box at the rear. A gong hangs under the footboard, and lanterns are substituted for lamps by the driver's seat, providing portable lights at the fire scene. Wine-color body and gear. Body decorated with gold leaf, and gear striped with gold and fine lines of orange. Wheels 38″ and 50″. *The Hub,* vol. 32, June 1890, pl. 20.

159

160

159. Hose reel. Hose was often carried on reels such as this one. All parts were brilliantly painted and decorated, the ends of the reel offering a large surface to the artist. Metal fittings were plated and highly polished. Manchester Locomotive Works, Manchester, New Hampshire, catalog of 1899, p. 25.

160. Hose cart. Hose reels were sometimes on two wheels. This one also carries a box at the rear and one under the driver's seat to carry fuel for the engine. Some larger fuel carts were also attached to the hose cart like a limber to an army gun carriage, creating a four-wheel vehicle. Amoskeag Mfg. Co., Manchester, New Hampshire, catalog of 1866, p. 40.

161

162

163

161. **Fire-patrol wagon.** This general-purpose utility vehicle featured a 20″-wide box in the center of the body to serve as a supply locker and a seat for firemen. There are additional lockers under the driving seat and under the body. A life net was carried in the cylinder behind the seat, and a fire extinguisher can be seen at the rear of the wagon. Firemen could also stand on the rear and side steps. Vermilion body, striped gold, with black chamfers. Vermilion gear, striped black. Brass mountings. Wheels 36″ and 51″. *The Hub,* vol. 41, May 1899, pl. 418.

162. **Combination chemical and hose wagon.** This wagon carried 600′ of 3″ hose, 800′ of 2½″ hose, nozzles and tools, portable fire extinguishers and the 60-gallon soda-acid tank under the driver's seat. The hose for the chemical tank is in the basket behind the acetylene searchlight. Two 10′ ladders were carried under the floor. Firemen could ride on the rear and side steps. *The Carriage Monthly,* vol. 41, July 1905, pl. 876.

163. **Police patrol wagon.** These wagons could be used to carry police officers to their place of duty, or as emergency vehicles, reporting to the scenes of fires, riots or accidents. Officers rode on wagonette-style benches, under which were lockers for such equipment as ropes, litters and first-aid supplies. Fire extinguishers were also occasionally carried. The four coil springs hanging in the passenger compartment supported a litter when the wagon was needed as an ambulance. Deep blue body, striped yellow. Yellow gear, striped deep blue. Wheels 41″ and 52″. *The Carriage Monthly,* vol. 49, July 1913, opposite p. 29.

164

165

164. Prison van. Popularly known as the "Black Maria" (although not always painted black), these vans transported prisoners to and from prison. The interior, usually lined with sheet iron, had a narrow, barred opening at the top for ventilation. This model has doors in the front, just behind the driver's seat; many had a rear door instead. Most had no benches inside. Tuscan red body and gear, the latter striped black. Wheels 36″ and 50″. *The Carriage Monthly*, vol. 22, March 1887, pl. 96.

165. Sprinkling wagon. To alleviate the dust nuisance on streets and roadways, various types of tank wagons sprinkled water on the surfaces. This wagon is of a less common design, intended for a special type of sprinkling. Built lighter in weight for use in parks, it had broad tires that would not cut the softer dirt and gravel surfaces of the park drives. An operator stood on the small back platform. Dark blue body with black chamfers, striped white. Vermilion gear, striped black with a fine line of white or yellow. Wheels 38″ and 54″. *The Carriage Monthly*, vol. 15, Feb. 1880, pl. 88.

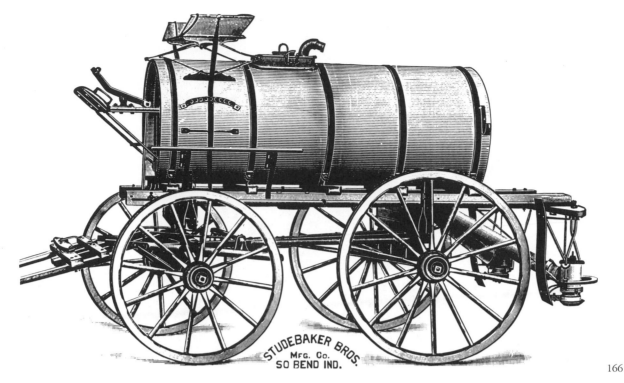

166

167

166. Sprinkling wagon. The more common sprinklers carried a cylindrical tank, such as the one shown here, on a small, one-horse-size body. It carried only 300 gallons; two-horse sizes ranged up to 1000 gallons. It is equipped with "Niagara" sprinkling heads, which were operated from the driver's seat and functioned independently, so that one of them could throw a heavy spray while the other threw a light spray to avoid wetting passing vehicles or pedestrians. Cream tank, striped red and blue, on a red gear, striped white. Studebaker Bros. Mfg. Co., South Bend, Indiana, catalog no. 181, 1901, p. 9.

167. Sprinkling cart. Here is a lighter, 150-gallon, sprinkler intended for use on private drives, or for watering lawns or crops. Its was equipped with twin sprinkling heads that could be adjusted to throw a spray 1'–18' wide, or they could be adjusted to two narrow sprays to water rows of crops. A hose could be attached to carry water to areas where the cart could not be driven. Green tank on a red gear. Wheels 54". Studebaker Bros. Mfg. Co., South Bend, Indiana, catalog no. 181, 1901, p. 30.

168

169

168. Road oiler. Tank wagons were also used to spread oil in the construction and maintenance of roads. Unlike the sprinklers, which threw the water in a wide, arching spray, these were designed to distribute the oil directly to the road in as short a vertical stream as possible, to avoid splashing passing vehicles, pedestrians or nearby property. Some, such as this, used gravity feed; others were pressurized, acting as an atomizer. Asphalt, binders and tar products could also be spread. This oiler has dual controls and can be operated either by the driver or a rear attendant. Studebaker Bros. Mfg. Co., South Bend, Indiana, catalog no. 298, 1909, p. 30.

169. Street sweeper. To maintain attractive and sanitary city streets, refuse had to be removed frequently, either by hand sweepers, flushing or by a sweeper such as this one. The rear axle drove a countershaft through a pair of bevel gears; final drive of the broom was by chain. Setting the broom at an angle made it sweep refuse toward the curb, where it was picked up by men with handcarts. For most satisfactory results, the sweeper was often preceded by the sprinkler, adjusted to give a fine sprinkling to keep down the dust. Studebaker Bros. Mfg. Co., South Bend, Indiana, catalog no. 298, 1909, p. 36.

170. Oil-tank wagon. Retail deliveries of oil and fuels were made from tank wagons similar to sprinkling wagons. Sizes carrying 300 to 1000 gallons were available. Most had internal dividers to form two or three separate compartments in the tank, which could carry lubricating oils, kerosene or gasoline, piped to the rear and dispensed from faucets inside the box. The box carried a measure and a funnel. Many wagons had racks on the sides, to carry additional oil or fuel in cans. Studebaker Bros. Mfg. Co., South Bend, Indiana, catalog no. 298, 1909, p. 31.

171

172

171. Caterpillar truck. In 1902, Alfred Kilby, of Dennysville, Maine, built this track-laying truck to carry loads over soft ground, the object being to distribute the weight over a larger area. The treads consist of metal cans attached to flat links at the sides. Each track runs around a series of four iron wheels secured between a pair of side plates. (Truck in the Smithsonian Institution.)

172. Caterpillar truck. George Hutton, of Richmond, Quebec, built this truck in 1905 and patented it in the United States and Canada. It differs from Kilby's in having tracks built of rollers instead of blocks. While devices like Hutton's and Kilby's performed satisfactorily, they did not enjoy widespread use before the introduction of the motor vehicle. (Photograph from the Smithsonian Institution.)

173

174

173. Road grader. For building and repairing roads, graders such as this one were used to smooth and level surfaces. Hand wheels operated worm-gear mechanisms to raise and lower the blade, which in this model could be had in lengths of 6′, 8′ and 10′. A scarifier attachment, fitted with ten sturdy teeth, could be mounted in front of the blade to assist in breaking up hard, uneven surfaces, enabling a more efficient action by the blade. Russell Grader Mfg. Co., Minneapolis, Minnesota, catalog of ca. 1926, p. 9.

174. Wagon loader and elevating grader. This machine does a bit more than no. 173. Instead of pushing the dirt aside, it scrapes the dirt up, raises it by conveyor and dumps it into a wagon running alongside. (Photograph from the Smithsonian Institution.)

175

175. Tree-transplanting wagon. This wagon is but one example of the many unusual vehicles constructed for special purposes. The lever-operated winches that raised the tree and its ball of earth are at both ends of the wagon, which could raise and carry a load of 14 tons. *Manufacturer and Builder,* May 1870.

176. Conestoga wagon. One of the more colorful and fascinating vehicles of the earlier period was this wagon, which plied the roads of Pennsylvania (later of Maryland and Ohio) from about 1750 to 1860. Not a wagon used for Westward migration, as is commonly believed, this was a freighter, carrying goods west from such cities as Philadelphia and Baltimore, and carrying material back to the point of origin

when drivers were fortunate enough to get a return load. Varying in size, they carried from one to five tons. This is a larger example in the Smithsonian Institution. (Photograph from the Smithsonian Institution.)

177. Conestoga wagon. Driven by professional "waggoners," the Conestogas were drawn by four to seven horses (many had a single leader). Using a single jerk line, rather than double lines, the driver variously rode the left-wheel horse or the lazy board near the left center of the wagon, or else walked. He did not ride inside. The box on the rear was used for feeding the horses, and the small box on the side was for tools. (Drawing, by John Thompson, of a wagon at the American Museum in Britain, Bath, England. Protected by copyright.)

96

176

177

178

179

178. Delivery wagon. These wagons formed the largest group of commercial vehicles, being built in many sizes and styles for all sorts of ordinary and specialized delivery work. Here is one of the common types, with straight bottom, panel sides and platform springs, adaptable to almost any kind of light or medium work. This one-horse wagon was available in three-quarter- or one-ton sizes, at $377 and $387, respectively. The small front wheels and full-circle fifth wheel permit sharp turning, but place the floor 41″ above the ground. Numerous color combinations were available. Wheels 36″ and 48″. Studebaker Bros. Mfg. Co., South Bend, Indiana, catalog no. 601, 1912, p. 75.

179. Delivery wagon. Often called a screen wagon because of the screened sides, this versatile vehicle, popular with department-store owners, has curtains rolled up to the roof. The curtains near the driving seat are separate from the main curtains. This example was built by George Lengert & Sons, a noted Philadelphia builder of such vehicles. Bottle green body, striped yellow; red center panel, striped white and gold. Red gear, striped black. Rubber-cloth trimings. Wheels 38″ and 53½″. *The Carriage Monthly,* vol. 26, Jan. 1891, pl. 77.

180. Delivery wagon. Finnesey & Kobler, another Philadelphia builder, constructed this attractive wagon. The polished hubcaps (covering the axle nuts), the roof railing and the stylish lamps helped to attract attention, suggesting quality in the products carried. The roof railing could be used to carry a larger load, but more likely was for effect only, for there is no step evident to facilitate loading the roof nor the usual wear strips to protect the roof fabric. (Photograph from the Smithsonian Institution.)

181

182

183

181. Dry-goods delivery wagon. More stylish in design, this two-horse wagon would have been used by one of the more progressive merchants, for its very execution advertises quality. The carriage-style seat, with its driving cushion, is unusual for this kind of wagon, and probably carried a neat, uniformed driver—a further indication of quality. The drop-center rear axle lowers the floor for ease in loading. White body panels, striped gold; light blue corner posts; center panel of rattan work with light blue behind it. Canary yellow gear, striped red. Wheels 42″ and 54″. *The Hub,* vol. 34, June 1892, pl. 17.

182. Delivery wagon. Less common in a vehicle of this class is the sloping floor of the truck, facilitating loading and unloading heavy materials. This one, designed for the wholesale paper trade, is ordinary in other respects. It was used with two

horses. Wheels 38″ and 52″. *The Hub,* vol. 32, Jan. 1891, pl. 74.

183. Delivery wagon. In another model, the wheelhouse under the driver's seat allowed sharper turning and permitted a slightly lower body for ease in loading. The single lamp, here used as a cyclops headlamp, is more decorative than functional. The street scene painted on the panel, while not entirely typical in subject matter, is an example of the paintings occasionally applied to a commercial vehicle to depict the location of the business that owned the vehicle. Yellow lower panels and seat panels; balance of body, black; center of the moldings on the yellow panels, striped black. Yellow gear, striped black. Gold mountings. Wheels 38″ and 48″. *The Carriage Monthly,* vol. 26, June 1890, pl. 24.

184. Delivery wagon. This tastefully designed cut-under wagon was used with two horses. The crescent-shaped lights, fitted with beveled glass, are mostly decorative, for they stand behind the driving seat. The dash is of wood, rather than patent leather—a fairly common feature on commercial vehicles. Deep green upper panels; lighter green lower panels; black moldings, striped gold. Nile green gear, striped carmine with fine lines of gold. Trimmings of green leather. Wheels 36″ and 48″. *The Hub,* vol. 38, Feb. 1897, pl. 281.

185. Florist's delivery wagon. Florists, or other business people who had attractive wares they wished to show off, often used wagons with glass sides. Here is one with low panels

topped by two beveled glass panes. Black body, striped gold. Carmine gear, striped black. Silver mountings. Trimmings of pebble leather. Wheels 35½″ and 48″. *The Hub,* vol. 37, Jan. 1896, pl. 204.

186. Light delivery wagon. The lightest delivery wagons, intended for small-parcel delivery, often resembled buggies or light phaetons with a small cargo box on the back. Mounted, like an ordinary buggy, on three elliptic springs, this one has a wheelhouse to make the wagon appear lighter, for the high front wheels do not pass entirely under it (note the rub iron). Canary yellow body with black moldings. Wine-color gear, striped yellow. Silver mountings. Wheels 40″ and 46″. *The Hub,* vol. 33, July 1891, pl. 21.

185

186

187

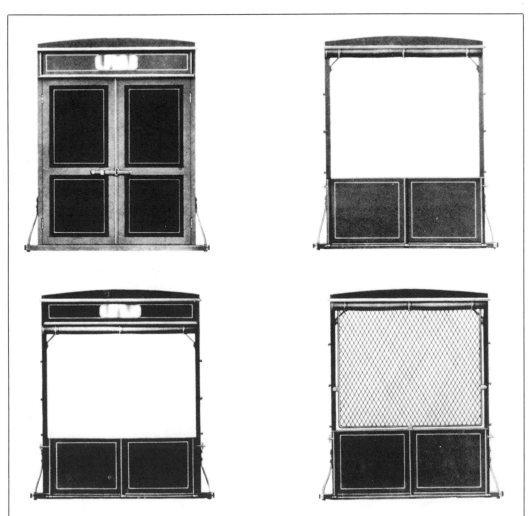

188

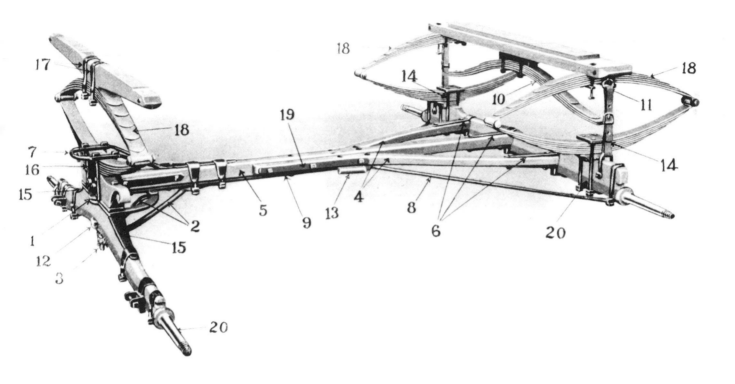

1. Forged D. & T. plates, male and female.
2. Double clipped forged drop stays.
3. Norway split head king bolt.
4. Bent wood hounds, long jaws.
5. Tapered reach.
6. Norway forged reach and hound clips.
7. Norway double spring brace and pole loop.
8. Iron stay braces.
9. Iron reach plate.
10. Check spring.

11. Check strap.
12. Swelled center axle.
13. Rolled steel rub iron.
14. Norway shrunk spring clips, bolts and plates.
15. Extension D plates.
16. Iron head block plate.
17. Norway forged spring bar clips.
18. Oil tempered steel springs.
19. Hound jaw plates.
20. Concord steel axles, increased arms.

189

187. Delivery wagon. This was called a phaeton-front wagon, because of the drop front. While it did not lower the cargo space, it did lower the driver's compartment, making it easier for him to get in and out during frequent calls. This is a wagon of small capacity (1200 pounds) and the cargo space is only 39" long and 43" wide. The wagon was available in many color combinations. Wheels 36" and 48". Studebaker Bros. Mfg. Co., South Bend, Indiana, catalog no. 601, 1912, p. 69.

188. Delivery-wagon ends. These were several options available for the rear ends of delivery wagons. The two on the left have small windows at the top. The screen at the lower right could be raised at any angle. Studebaker Bros. Mfg. Co., South Bend, Indiana, catalog no. 601, 1912, p. 12.

189. Delivery-wagon running gear. Here is a common three-spring gear used on many one-horse delivery wagons. Studebaker Mfg. Co., South Bend, Indiana, catalog no. 601, 1912, p. 10.

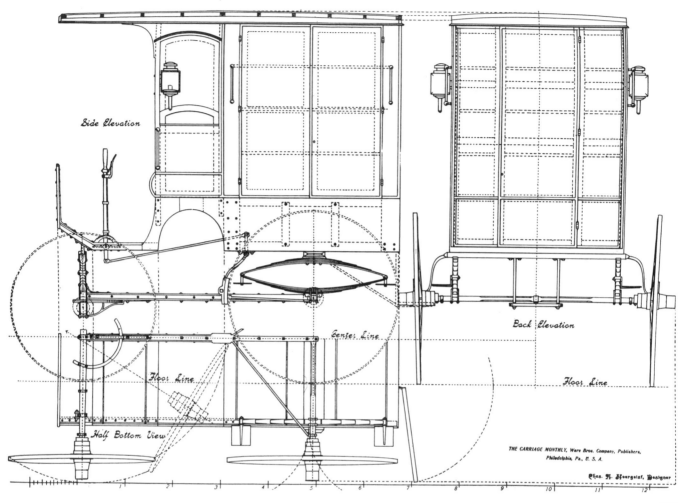

Side Elevation

Back Elevation

Center Line

Floor Line

Floor Line

Half Bottom View

THE CARRIAGE MONTHLY, Ware Bros. Company, Publishers,
Philadelphia, Pa., U. S. A.

Chas. N. Heergeist, Designer

190

190. Library wagon. Washington County Library, in Hagerstown, Maryland, is said to have been the first library to offer a traveling-library service to its citizens. A wagon similar to this one was used to carry books to readers in all parts of the county in days when Americans did not have the freedom of movement we know today. Doors opened on both sides, in front and rear, to expose many shelves full of books. The steps attached to both ends of the springs assisted one in reaching books. Wheels 36″ and 42″. *The Carriage Monthly,* vol. 46, July 1910, p. 25.

191. Delivery wagon. Some businessmen requested carriage builders to construct wagons that were better adapted to their special needs. This wagon was designed for hotel service, carrying the trunks and luggage of guests and, on occasion, hotel supplies. The style of a fine carriage was maintained in front, while the floor is dropped in back for loading ease. This was accomplished through the use of smaller wheels and half-elliptic springs in the rear, the front springs being the usual platform type. English vermilion body and gear; body, blocked off in black and striped white. Gear striped black with fine lines of white. Wheels 32″ and 40″. *The Carriage Monthly,* vol. 16, March 1881, pl. 95.

192. Delivery wagon. Fashionable businesses often chose vehicle designs that reflected elegance and dignity. This two-horse wagon on four elliptic springs has a stylish body and a carriage-style driving seat. The driving cushion (the raised, sloping cushion on the right) almost certainly dictates a uniformed driver. The wagon was built by the prominent Kean and Lines, of New Haven, Connecticut, then one of the nation's leading carriage-building centers. Black upper part of body and boot; deep sea-green lower panel; gold lettering. Deep sea-green gear. Dark green morocco trimmings. Gold mountings. Wheels 36″ and 42″. *The Carriage Monthly,* vol. 19, Dec. 1883, pl. 75.

191

192

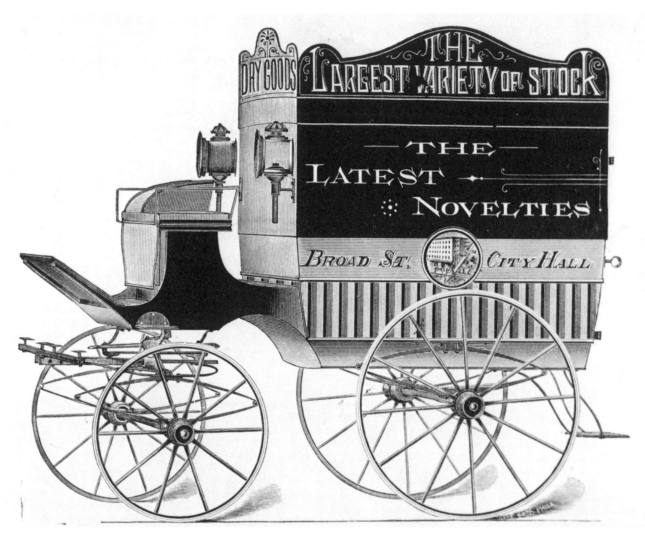

193. Delivery wagon. This stylish design, with the coach-type boot and driving cushion, provides a larger cargo space. A helper dressed in livery rode on the back. Black upper panels with gold lettering; black boot and panels above top; primrose yellow center panel with black letters; primrose yellow lower panels, striped dark and light cherry red (¾" stripe). Primrose yellow gear with two joining stripes of dark and light cherry red. Brass mountings. Wheels 37" and 50". *The Carriage Monthly,* vol. 20, Aug. 1884, pl. 40.

194. Delivery wagon. While this ample-sized body is entirely ordinary in style, the fore and aft seats, for driver and helper, suggest a fine road coach or park drag, to attract the attention of the "carriage trade." Better still, it might suggest to others that, if you dealt with Mawson's, you were associated with that class. The height of the seats was less considerate of driver and helper. Yellow lake body with black moldings, roof and round corners; blue diamond edges of moldings; top edges of moldings striped gold; black lettering, shaded gold. Dark blue gear, striped gold. Brown leather trimmings. Wheels 38" and 53". *The Carriage Monthly,* vol. 20, June 1884, pl. 20.

195. Delivery wagon. Based on an ordinary cut-under design, this colorful wagon has lines in its rear portion that are reminiscent of a coupé body to suggest class. (Strawbridge & Clothier continues to serve Philadelphians.) Orange-yellow upper and lower panels and front; cream center panels and boards on top; light green slats; lighter yellow coupé pillar and corresponding area in rear. Orange-yellow gear, striped black. Trimmings of enamel leather and a green carpet. Wheels 36" and 47". *The Carriage Monthly,* vol. 20, Sept. 1884, pl. 48.

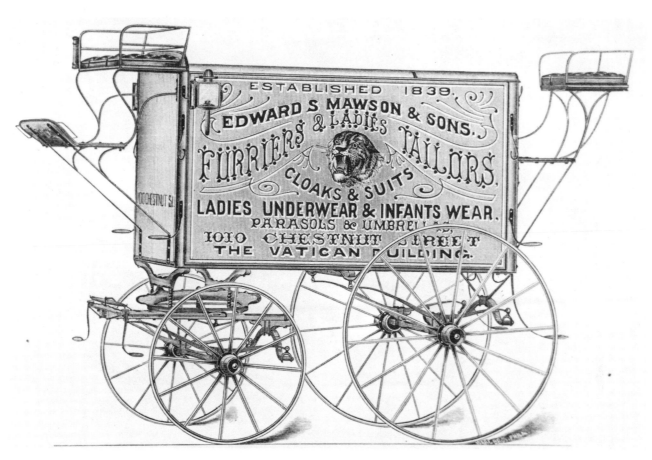

194

195

196

THIS DESIGN IS PATENTED

Fulton & Walker
Company
Builders.

PHILADELPHIA, U.S.A.

WARE BROS   PHILA

198

196. Delivery wagon. An attractively designed cut-under wagon of a fairly ordinary design, this model sports an unusual canopy top and interesting wire sides. It was used by a dealer in wirework such as wire baskets, pet cages, etc. White body; dark brown plaited work; panels striped gold and brown; blue wirework with gold frame and scrollwork. Carmine gear, striped with black lines, one broad and two fine. Black enameled-cloth trimmings for cushion and fall; dark brown cloth for the head lining. Gold mountings. Wheels 37″ and 47″. *The Hub,* vol. 28, May 1886, pl. 15.

197. Delivery wagon. This attempt to follow the lines of a coach was intended for grocery and small-parcel delivery. While the effect is questionable, the design appears to have been more satisfactory for frequent calls, for it features the drop-center of the milk or baker's wagon, which made the

driver's life somewhat easier. Driven from the rear or from a central standing position if desired, the lines rested on the rail seen in the front opening. Dark green body with black moldings, striped carmine. Carmine gear, striped black. Wheels 37″ and 48″. *The Hub,* vol. 28, Sept. 1886, pl. 50.

198. Delivery wagon. Another effort to imitate carriage design is this otherwise ordinary wagon, built with curved rails and a very slight side swell to accentuate the effect. The design was patented (unusual for an entire vehicle design) by the well-known builder of commercial work, the Fulton and Walker Company of Philadelphia. White body; gold beveled edges on upper and lower moldings; red drip molding; center and upper panels striped light blue. White gear, striped dark blue with fine lines in light blue. Wheels 36″ and 50″. *The Carriage Monthly,* vol. 29, Sept. 1892, pl. 46.

199. Advertising-delivery wagon. While all lettered vehicles advertised, there were numerous exciting and colorful deviations from the usual designs, intended to attract attention as well as to carry goods. More common in the larger cities, some carried only minimal loads, heavier shipments being sent in the conventional wagons. Because of the small size of the product, this wagon probably advertised and delivered. Tobacco-brown cigar body; red label; carmine seat. Carmine gear, striped black and white. Wheels 36″ and 46″. *The Hub,* vol. 33, Jan. 1892, pl. 59.

200. Advertising-delivery wagon. This cigar wagon is less novel in appearance, but larger in capacity. The falling top can be pushed back, but obviously not folded down; it was probably always used as shown. Tobacco-brown cigars; balance of the body and the gear, London smoke. Green leather trimming. Wheels 38″ and 46″. *The Hub,* vol. 34, Aug. 1892, pl. 30.

201. Advertising-delivery cart. A novel two-wheeler, this was used for a hatter's deliveries. The driving seat is recessed into the top of the crown. A hat, in its individual box, takes sufficient space to make this vehicle impractical if the hatter had a substantial business. For deliveries, a larger vehicle may have supplemented this attention-getter. Black hat with a carmine sweatband, and toeboard. Carmine gear, striped black. Wheels 48″. *The Hub,* vol. 32, Sept. 1890, pl. 47.

200

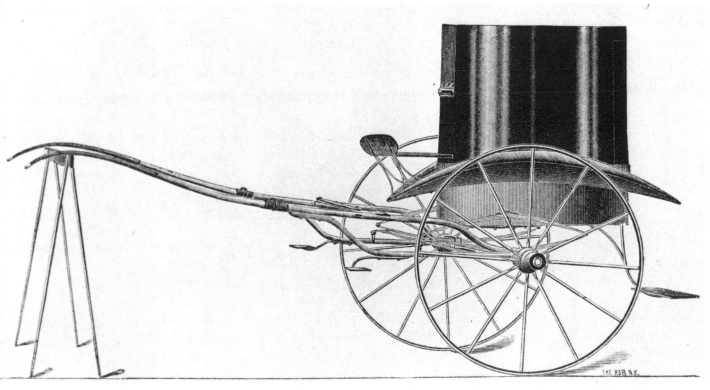

201

202

203

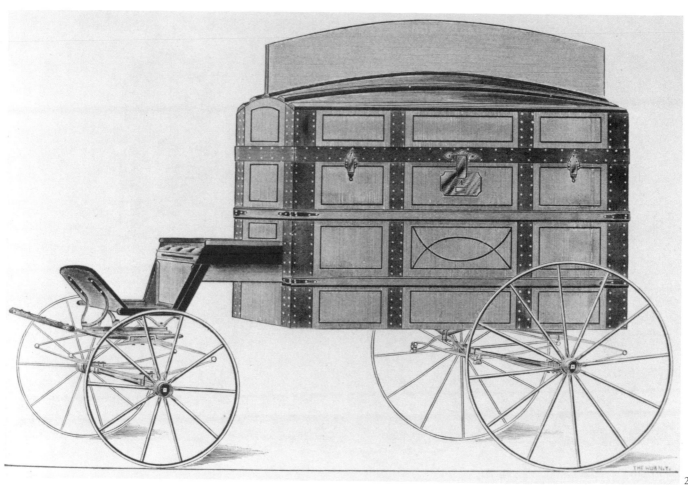

204

202. Advertising-delivery cart. The small size of the product and the moderate size of the body made this jeweler's cart more practical. The builder reported that he used bent wheel rims to frame the body. Blue body; gilded moldings and bail handle on top; gold lettering with carmine border. White gear, striped carmine. Gold mountings. Wheels 63″. *The Hub,* vol. 30, July 1888, pl. 32.

203. Advertising-delivery wagon. A luggage dealer's suitcase on wheels, the vehicle had a center panel large enough to carry his lettering. The cyclops headlamp was more for effect than for use. Black body with gold ornamentation. Vermilion gear, glazed carmine with black and gold striping. Silver mountings. Wheels 36″ and 50″. *The Carriage Monthly,* vol. 18, June 1882, pl. 24.

204. Advertising-delivery wagon. The builder constructed a camel-back trunk of ample size for trunk delivery. The topboard carried the lettering. Natural wood trunk with black irons and seat. Carmine gear, striped black. Black enamel-leather trimmings. Silver mountings. Wheels 36″ and 50″. *The Hub,* vol. 28, Aug. 1886, pl. 41.

205. **Advertising-delivery wagon.** Moxie was a popular soft drink. This wagon, on four heavy elliptic springs, is an example of an advertising-delivery wagon that could carry a heavy load. Curtains could be let down to cover the sides. The steps on the sides facilitated center loading and unloading. White body; side panels are plate-glass mirrors, with "Moxie" in gold, shaded blue; bottles painted to represent filled Moxie bottles; top panels dark lake with 6″ sheet-metal letters. White gear, striped red. Silver mountings. Wheels 40″ and 52″. *The Hub,* vol. 39, Aug. 1897, pl. 317.

206. **Advertising-delivery wagon.** This two-horse wagon could carry two upright pianos back-to-back and four men for handling them—two on the driving seat and two on the

unusual side rumble seats. Lake body, striped gold and carmine. Vermilion gear, striped black. Wheels 40″ and 49″. *The Hub,* vol. 31, Jan. 1890, pl. 75.

207. **Advertising-delivery wagon.** Rather than displaying wares in the design, some wagons presented a symbol of the trade, such as the mortar and pestle on this druggist's wagon. Since druggists' goods are usually very small, the parcels were carried in the box under the seat, and there is no indication in the description that the mortar and pestle are any more than a sham. Black body, striped gold and green. Vermilion gear, striped black. Wheels 42″ and 47″. *The Hub,* vol. 32, Nov. 1890, pl. 58.

206

207

208. Advertising-delivery wagon. An unusual wagon by McCabe, Young & Co., of St. Louis, Missouri, which constructed a number of such vehicles. The design was particularly appropriate for any firm using the word "Globe" or "World" in its name. The globe, five feet in the diameter and finished with gold and silver leaf, was accessible through double doors that opened over the driver's seat. The horse was ornamented with bells that had outside clappers. Wheels 40″ and 48″. *The Hub,* vol. 32, July 1890, p. 9.

209. Advertising-delivery wagon. A spectacular wagon, this uses the cyclops headlamp for effect. The brakes for this heavy load were operated by a handwheel. Bright yellow "circulation" panel with black lettering; black "Times" panel with gold lettering shaded red; azure blue earth panel with gray earth shaded black, gold lettering shaded blue and black "1890" shaded green; deep blue main panels with white lettering shaded green; black lower panel; new copper-color cent on a yellow background; blue frame of front door; black sides of boot; yellow front with black lettering. Blue gear, striped white. Gold mountings. Wheels 36″ and 48″. *The Carriage Monthly,* vol. 26, Jan. 1891, pl. 79.

210. Advertising-delivery wagon. A wagon such as this could be used by a business such as a novelty shop or an exotic-food dealer. The wagon is basically rather ordinary, but the profile and artwork are unusual. The brilliant painting was surrounded by moldings of carmine and vermilion. Carmine gear, striped gold with fine white lines. Silver mountings and bells at the four corners. Wheels 38″ and 52″. *The Carriage Monthly,* vol. 23, Nov. 1887, pl. 69.

209

210

213

211. Advertising-delivery wagon. This is another rather ordinary wagon made unusual by its decoration. Of ample size, it was capable of carrying a substantial load—in this instance, of preserved fruit, as suggested by several motifs. Light cream upper panels; dark blue rear corner panels and lower panels; artwork brilliantly colored. Dark blue gear, striped with a ½" line of black. *The Carriage Monthly,* vol. 21, Apr. 1885, p. 10.

212. Advertising-delivery wagon. Not all advertising-delivery wagons were unusual in design or decoration. Here is one that differs from a regular delivery wagon only in that it is slightly less than half size. This one was used by a veterinarian in Washington, D.C., to pick up an occasional sick or injured dog, but was mostly driven about the streets by Robinson's two young sons, Joseph and Charles, merely to attract attention. The wagon and the 1897 photo were given to the Smithsonian

Institution by Joseph F. Robinson (standing at the rear wheel) in 1972. Black with gold lettering, on a deep red unstriped gear.

213. Advertising-delivery wagon. When the veterinary ambulance shown in no. 212 was restored, an earlier layer of paint was found underneath the black, revealing that the original owner had been a bakery. Again, the vehicle was used only for effect, for the Connecticut Pie Company operated a substantial fleet of large wagons on Washington's streets. Because of this interesting discovery, when the wagon was recently restored, one side was finished with Robinson's decor; the other with the pie company's. A foot-operated bell is under the toeboard. Deep red body; gold letters outlined in yellow and shaded variously in two of the colors green, red and orange; striped gold and black. Lighter red gear, striped black, white and yellow. (Photograph from the Smithsonian Institution.)

214

215

214. Advertising-vending wagon. This large wagon was a portable store, by the famed wagon builder, Fulton and Walker, of Philadelphia. The side shown here has plate-glass windows, while the other side is paneled, and carried a painting of people, premiums offered and bees (in reference to Colgate's Bee Soap and Bee Washing Powder). Inside, the 21′-long, 7½′-high body had four 12″ shelves to display the merchandise. Lettering covered the lower panel. Red gear, striped black. Wheels 39″ and 54″. *The Carriage Monthly,* vol. 34, May 1898, pl. 9.

215. Mail-collector's cart. Two-wheelers such as this one were used in New York and other cities to collect mail from drop boxes. Despite the cart's size, its cargo space was substantial.

Red upper panels and seat; white center panels; blue lower panels; gold striping. Yellow gear, striped vermilion. Wheels 51½″. *The Hub,* vol. 38, Nov. 1896, pl. 264.

216. Mail-collector's wagon. The carts used in New York City's business districts were replaced by these wagons, built by the Abbot, Downing Co. Having a large cargo space, the vehicle required a driver and a collector, the latter riding at the back, with a speaking tube to communicate with the driver. The drop-center axle eased the burden of carrying mail into the wagon. Carmine top panels, striped gold; white belt panels, striped red; blue lower panels, striped gold. Yellow gear, striped with ¼″-wide red line and with fine lines of blue. Wheels 36″ and 50″. *The Hub,* vol. 43, Dec. 1901, pl. 539.

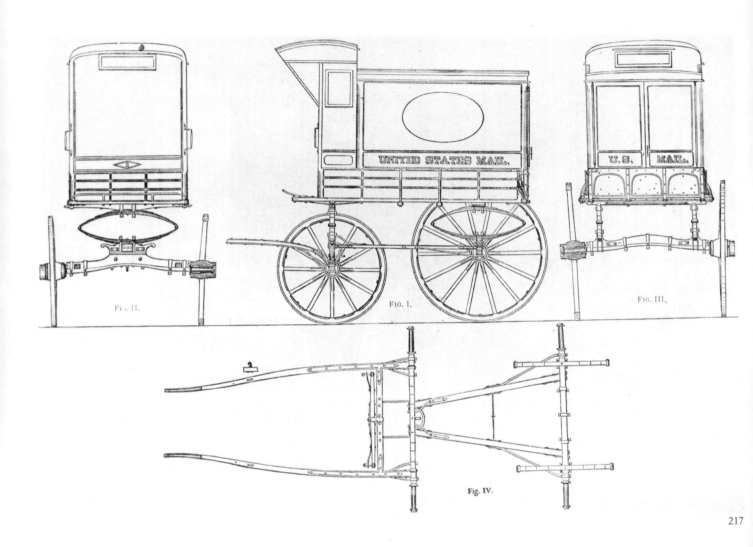

FIG. II.   FIG. I.   FIG. III.

Fig. IV.

UNITED STATES MAIL.   U.S. MAIL.

217

217. Mail wagon. In addition to this one-horse wagon, two-horse sizes were also used for bulk movement of mailbags between depot and post office, and to branch post offices. Later wagons had the screen sides seen on many delivery wagons. Blue lower body, finely striped with red and white; white lettering panels; red upper panels and doors; gold-leaf lettering, shaded with two shades of carmine; the oval contained a crest showing a postboy, train, steamboat and telegraph. Light cream gear with broad vermilion stripe and two fine lines of blue. Wheels 41″ and 52″. *The Hub,* vol. 22, May 1880, pl. 20B.

218. Mail wagon. Popularly known as a "screen wagon" because of its screened sides, this regulation U.S. Mail Wagon, Size No. 1, was approved in 1904. Drawn by two horses, it carried 5000 pounds. It has sliding center doors at the sides, accessible by the side steps, and rear doors, behind which closes a tailgate used for loading and unloading only. Blue body, striped white; black chamfers, bolt and rivet heads; white flareboards and window panels, striped gold; gold lettering, shaded black. Red gear, striped with black and two fine white lines. Wheels 36″ and 52″. *Specifications for U.S. Mail Wagons,* Post Office Dept., Government Printing Office, Washington, D.C., 1904.

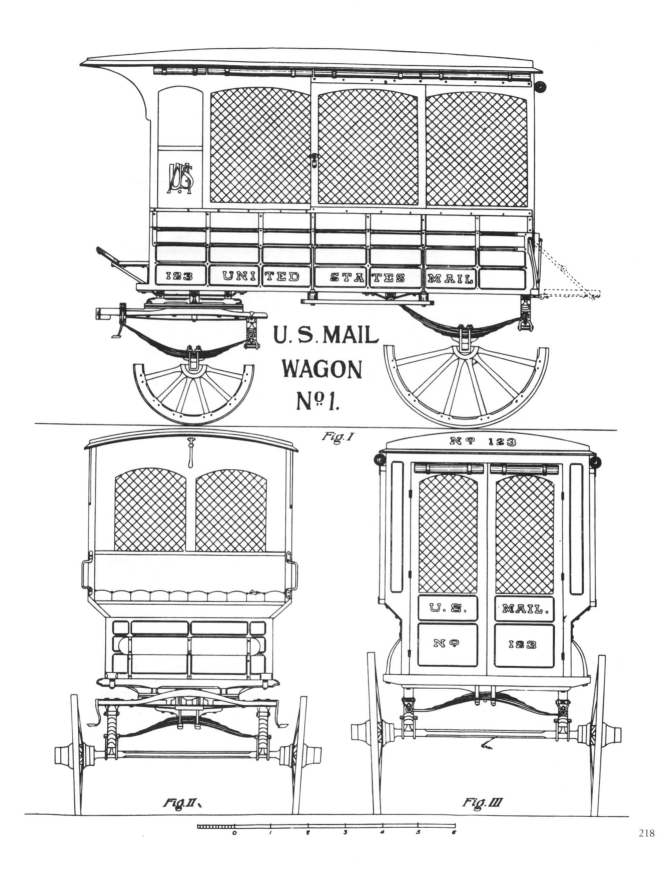

U. S. MAIL
WAGON
Nº 1.

Fig. I

Nº 123

U. S.   MAIL.

Nº   123

Fig. II

Fig. III

123 UNITED STATES MAIL

0   1   2   3   4   5   6

219. Rural mail wagon. This wagon, used for rural mail delivery, is still remembered. Small and light, usually with painted duck sides, this two-spring wagon had a seat, a desk with drawer and a number of pigeonholes. Some wagons had a small stove for winter use; a rear luggage rack was often added for parcel delivery. The doors slid to the rear. A large front light could be raised; when it was lowered, the driving lines passed through slots in the bottom of the frame. Blue lower body; white upper; red gear. Wheels 40″ and 44″. *The Carriage Monthly,* vol. 38, June 1902, pl. 600.

220. Carriage-builder's delivery wagon. These specialized wagons were developed by carriage builders for picking up such items as paints, small parts and supplies, and for delivering replacement parts to customers. The hooks on the pillars carried poles and shafts, and a box under the seat held small parcels. While none are evident on this wagon, under the rear of the body, many had hooks that were used to tow damaged vehicles in for repairs. Green body with gold striping and lettering; black moldings, striped gold. Vermilion gear, striped black and gold. Wheels 36″ and 48″. *The Hub,* vol. 36, July 1894, pl. 93.

221. Bill-posting wagon. This special-purpose wagon was used by the American Bill Posting Co., of Brooklyn, New York. Built with a touch of class in the front, the rearmost compartment appears awkward, since it was dropped lower to make the paste container more accessible. Brushes were carried under the seat, and bills were carried behind the seat in a compartment fitted with a storm cover. Vermilion body and gear, striped black. Wheels 36″ and 48″. *The Hub,* vol. 36, Feb. 1895, pl. 137.

220

AMERICAN
BILL POSTING CO

221

222

223

222. Butcher's wagon. Traveling butchers carried their meats, fish and oysters right to the homes of their customers. This wagon is typical in construction, having an upper endgate that raises to serve as a protective awning above the meats inside. The butcher could stand inside, to the left; on the right rear is a storage chest, on top of which is a cutting block. Shelves could be built to one side, and large meats hung on the other. Seafood was frequently carried under the driving seat. *The Blacksmith and Wheelwright,* Feb. 1904, p. 61.

223. Market wagon. The Buckeye Wagon Works, of Dayton, Ohio, produced this novel vehicle, designed to protect a huckster's produce arranged for public view behind the wagon. A secondary roof was moved backward, and the lightweight duck-covered sides were raised to serve as awnings. Then the

huckster had to hope for the absence of strong winds. Sliding doors are in the front. *The Carriage Monthly,* vol. 42, Jan. 1907, pl. 1019.

224. Milk wagon. A common special-purpose delivery wagon was that intended for regular door-to-door delivery of milk and bakery goods, the same designs being practical for both. This example is a slightly unusual variation, for the rear of the body presents a phaetonlike profile, while the front has a flaring dash. The wagon has the sliding door frequently used in these vehicles, and a cash drawer under the seat. Lake lower panels; carmine center panels with gilded scrollwork; white upper panels. Straw-color gear, striped black. Silver mountings. Wheels 35″ and 48″. *The Hub,* vol. 28, Jan. 1887, pl. 82.

225

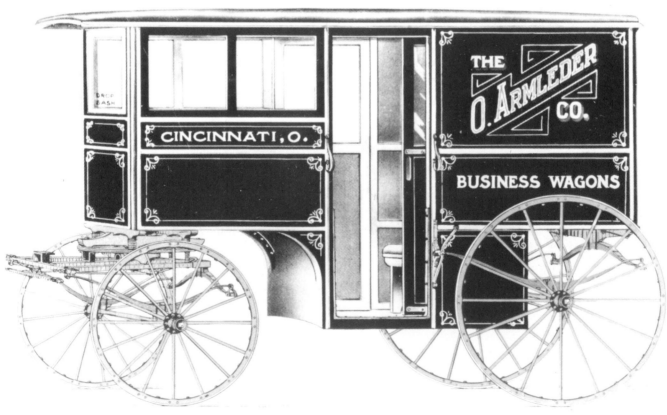

226

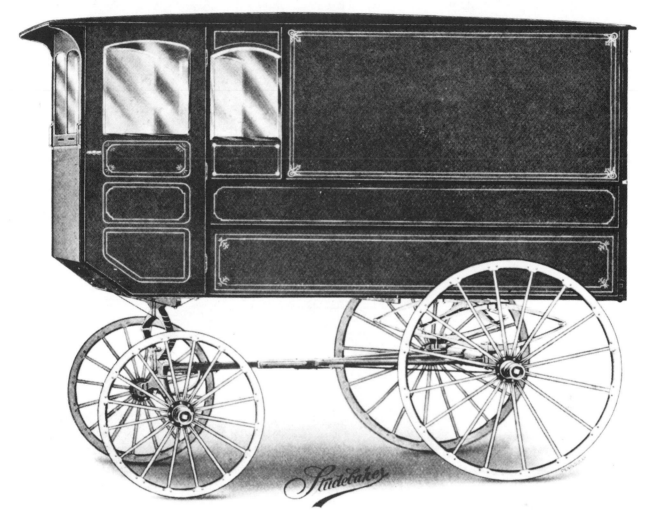

225. Milk or bakery wagon. Here is one of the more popular designs for this type of wagon, offered in 1000- and 1200-pound capacities, at prices from $180 to $200. It featured the usual sliding doors and a raising front sash, on the underside of which can be seen the small slot for the driving lines. The rear end has double doors for ease in loading. Upper-rear panels are duck painted red with yellow striping; green body, striped gold. Carmine gear, striped black. Wheels 38″ and 42″. Studebaker Bros. Mfg. Co., South Bend, Indiana, catalog no. 601, 1912, p. 37.

226. Milk or bakery wagon. A style that became highly popular in the later period was the drop-center wagon, which made access easier for the driver, who did not have to step high. It also allowed the front wheels to cut under for sharper turning. Like the previous wagon, it has rear doors, but the front sash drops into the body. The heavier suspension on platform springs increases the capacity to 1400–1800 pounds. These wagons were often painted in light colors better to reflect the heat of the sun. Cream was popular, and at a later period white was also frequently used. Wheels 34″ and 44″. O. Armleder Co., Cincinnati, Ohio, catalog, ca. 1918, p. 30.

227. Milk or bakery wagon. Here is a larger wagon of 2000-pound capacity that is more suited to wholesale delivery to stores. It is not easy to get in and out, for the floor is nearly four feet from the ground. The wagon has shelves inside, the usual doors in the rear, and doors between the cargo space and the driving seat. Dark green body with a red name panel. Red gear, striped black. Wheels 36″ and 50″. Studebaker Bros. Mfg. Co., South Bend, Indiana, catalog no. 223, 1903, p. 48.

228

229

228. Milk wagon. A still heavier wagon for wholesale milk delivery was used by New York City milk dealers. It could carry cases of bottles or large milk cans. The center steps assist in loading and unloading the center portion of the wagon. The standing fixtures are for tie-downs. Cream body, striped carmine with fine black lines. Carmine gear, striped black. Wheels 35″ and 50½″. *The Hub,* vol. 38, Nov. 1896, pl. 265.

229. Delivery wagon. Many delivery wagons were open vehicles similar to this attractively styled example, which provides cover for the driver. Open delivery wagons were far more common than is suggested by the comparatively few shown in this volume; more closed wagons are shown simply because they offered more opportunity for variations. Dark brown body, striped gold. Light brown gear, striped yellow. Brown trimmings. Wheels 35″ and 40″. *The Hub,* vol. 28, Jan. 1887, pl. 81.

230

231

230. Delivery wagon. A Singer wagon, with its coach-boot driving seat, presents an unusually elegant appearance for an open wagon, the lamps adding to the effect. Four elliptic springs and the two-horse draft suggest a moderately heavy load, although the two horses might have been used to increase the effect. The silver-plated rails on the sides serve only as ornaments. Wheels 37″ and 48″. *The Hub,* vol. 23, March 1882, pl. 148.

231. Delivery wagon. A most popular and versatile open style, widely used by merchants, contractors, grocers and hucksters, this could be used with one or two horses, carried 1000 pounds and cost $92. Options included flareboards, a low duck top and brakes. Dark green body, striped gold, with black irons. Gear red, striped black, or yellow, striped red. Wheels 40″ and 44″. Studebaker Bros. Mfg. Co., South Bend, Indiana, catalog no. 601, 1912. p. 47.

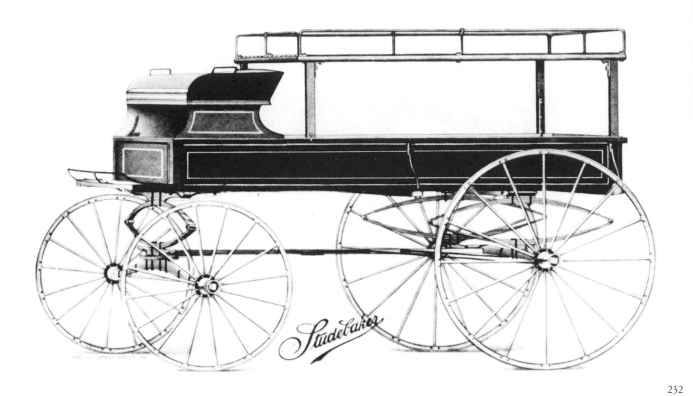

232

233

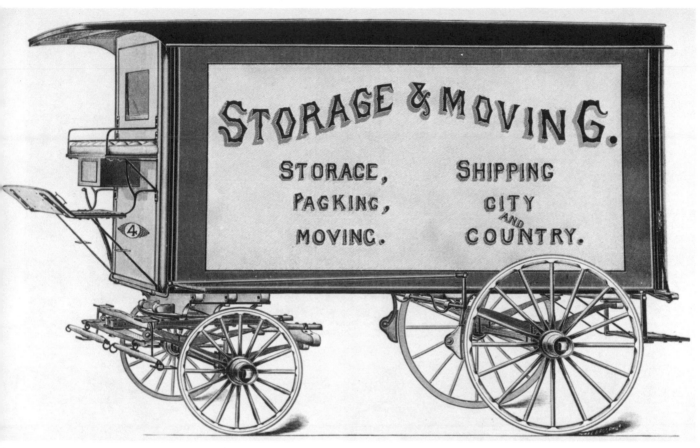

234

232. Delivery wagon. Although this is similar to the previous wagon. it differs in several respects. The front axle is arched and the diameter of the front wheels is decreased to give the cut-under feature for maneuverability. This raises the floor about 6″ higher than that of the other wagon. A second deck is also added, with iron railing, to increase the capacity without congesting the load. Painted the same as the previous wagon or a black body, striped gold, on a red gear, striped black. Wheels 34″ and 44″. Studebaker Bros. Mfg. Co., South Bend, Indiana, catalog no. 601, 1912, p. 55.

233. Platform spring wagon. While this serviceable vehicle could be used as a passenger wagon, as shown, with the rear seat removed, it was often employed as a delivery wagon. Priced at $51.50, it was the most economical delivery wagon to be had. The 8½′ body could carry 1200 pounds on 1⅛″ axles, or

1500 pounds on 1¼″ axles. Black body, striped gold. Dark Brewster green gear, striped red. Elkhart Carriage & Harness Mfg. Co., Elkhart, Indiana, catalog of 1907, p. 169.

234. Moving van. This heavier type of delivery vehicle is a cross between a truck and a delivery wagon. On truck springs and with the high driving seat of a truck, the large body, similar to that of an ordinary delivery wagon, could accommodate a substantial load of furniture. In spite of the size of this van, by Fulton and Walker of Philadelphia, the low front wheels permitted a high degree of maneuverability. Deep blue body, striped light blue, with gold lettering, shaded red (or silver lettering, shaded green). Lake gear, striped deep brown. Wheels 37″ and 54″. *The Carriage Monthly,* vol. 27, Aug. 1891, pl. 39.

235. Paper-box van. Other large van-type vehicles were built for special purpsoes, such as this paper-box van, which carried bulky, but not excessively heavy, loads. This one has the added feature of a top rail to hold overflow loads. Doors are in the sides only; most similar vehicles had the conventional rear doors. The low driving seat of the common delivery wagon was also frequently seen on these larger wagons. Blue body, striped gold and white. Red gear, striped black. Wheels 36″ and 48″. *The Hub,* vol. 33, Jan. 1892, pl. 62.

236. Furniture wagon. A most unusual furniture dealer's wagon, by L. S. Burr and Co., of Memphis, Tennessee, had an excessively long body. Nearly 19′, it must have created turning problems in crowded areas, although the high wheel-arch

somewhat alleviated the problem, while permitting large front wheels for easier draft. Graceful iron side braces extended upward from the sills. Wheels 50″ and 53″. *The New York Coach-maker's Magazine,* vol. 2, May 1860, pl. 40.

237. Furniture wagon. More conventional in design and suggesting an express wagon, this attractive and serviceable wagon was intended for a retail furniture dealer. The suspension is slightly unusual because it has the common platform springs in front but half elliptics in the rear. The iron loops on the endgate serve as steps when the gate is dropped. Black body, striped gold. Yellow gear, striped black. Wheels 36″ and 50″. *The Hub,* vol. 34, March 1893, pl. 70.

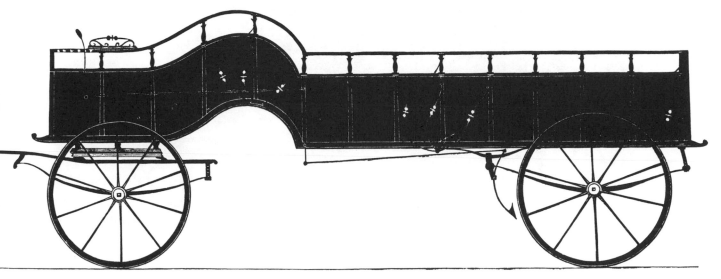

236

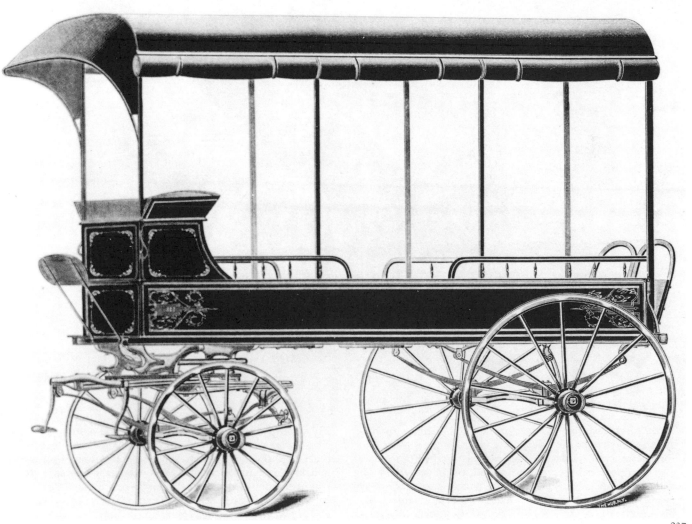

237

238. Dump wagon. Contractors, road builder, farmers—anyone who hauled materials that could be dumped—had need for wagons such as this one. The load was dumped, by means of a lever or pedal release, through the bottom of the wagon. The driver could draw up the twin doors from his seat as he drove away. Capacity was one and a half or two cubic yards. Green body. Yellow gear. Wheels 36″ and 50″. Columbia Wagon and Body Co., Columbia, Pennsylvania, catalog of ca. 1908, p. 24.

239. Dump wagon. Another style used end-dumping action. The brakes were set on the rear wheels and the team was backed up, shortening the wheelbase until gravity tipped the unbalanced body backwards. Then, when the operator drove forward with the brakes still set, the running gear was lengthened to normal, restoring balance. The Haywood Wagon Co., Newark, New York, catalog, ca. 1910, p. 20.

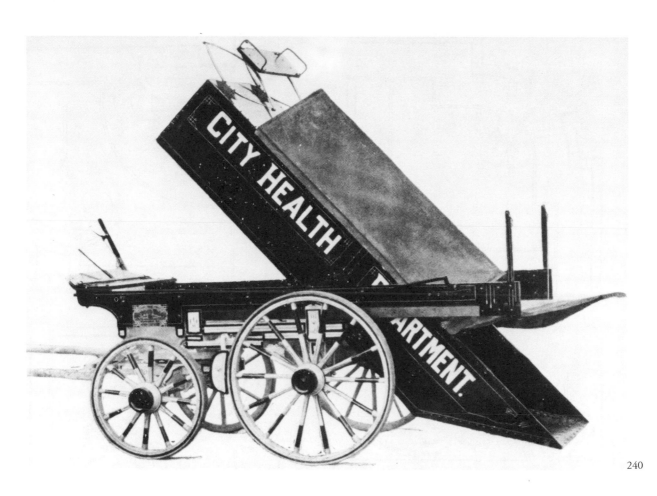

240

241

240. Dumping garbage wagon. Here is another end dumper by the same builder. Since it was intended to carry wet garbage and had to be leakproof, the body was of watertight steel construction. Thus it could not have an endgate, which would have leaked. The Haywood Wagon Co., Newark, New York, catalog, ca. 1910, p. 38.

241. Spreading (or distributing) wagon. This wagon is designed to dump its load gradually, at a controlled rate, across the width of the wagon. It was used for building broken-stone roads and for grading. Everything was controlled from the driver's seat. Wheels 40″ and 52″. Julian Scholl & Co., New York City, catalog of ca. 1900, p. 23.

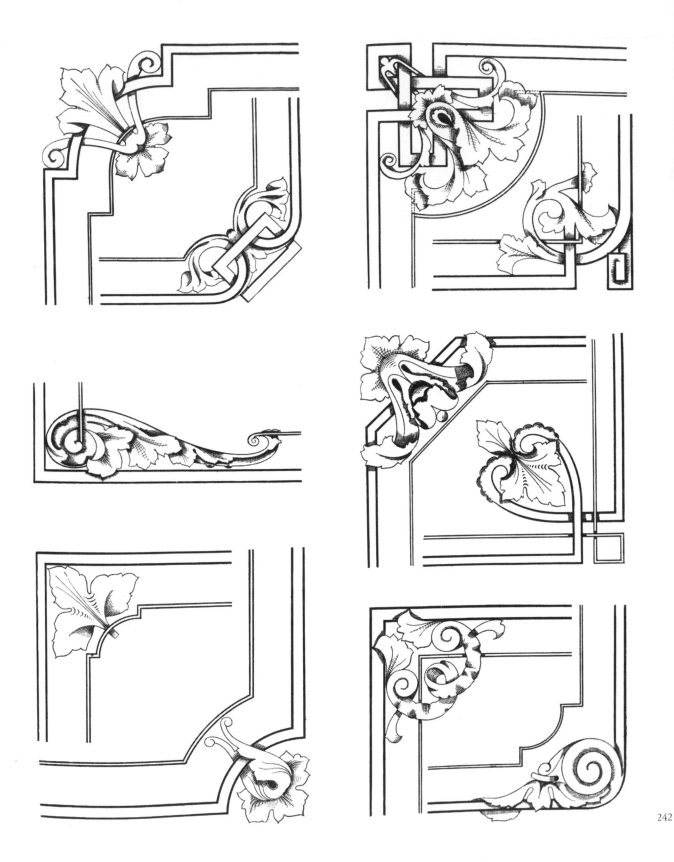

242

242. Panel designs. Known in the trade as corner-pieces, these designs were used to decorate the corners of panels on commercial vehicles. The stripes incorporated into the designs extended the length and width of the panels, joining designs in the four corners. *The Hub,* vol. 32, Dec. 1890, p. 709.

243. Panel designs. Additional lower panel designs show more corner-pieces, two seat riser designs and designs for belt panels, posts and footboards. *The Hub,* vol. 32, July 1890, p. 282; *The Carriage Monthly,* vol. 41, Nov. 1905, pp. 258 & 261.

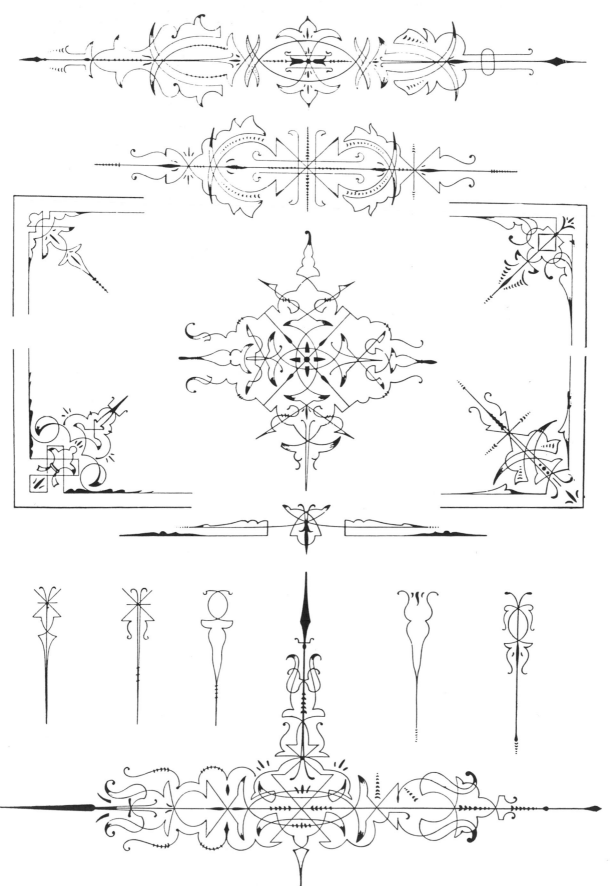

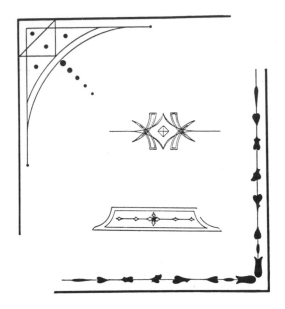

For Corners and Risers.

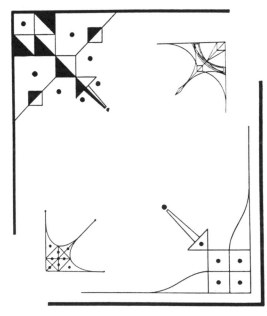

Corner Pieces for Upper and Lower Wagon Panels.

Automobile and Wagon Panel Finish.

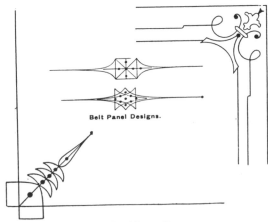

Belt Panel Designs.

Wagon Panel Corner Pieces.

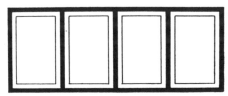

Automobile Design for Lower Wagon Panels.

Design for Lower Wagon Panel.

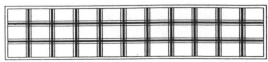

Latest Design for Automobile Panels.

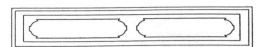

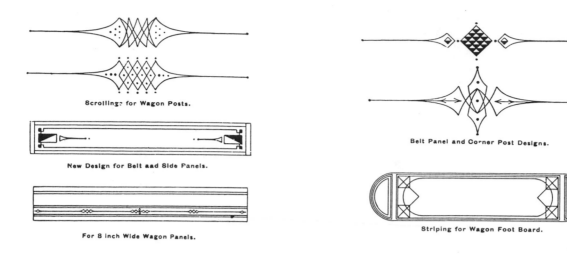

Scrolling for Wagon Posts.

New Design for Belt and Side Panels.

For 8 inch Wide Wagon Panels.

Belt Panel and Corner Post Designs.

Striping for Wagon Foot Board.

244

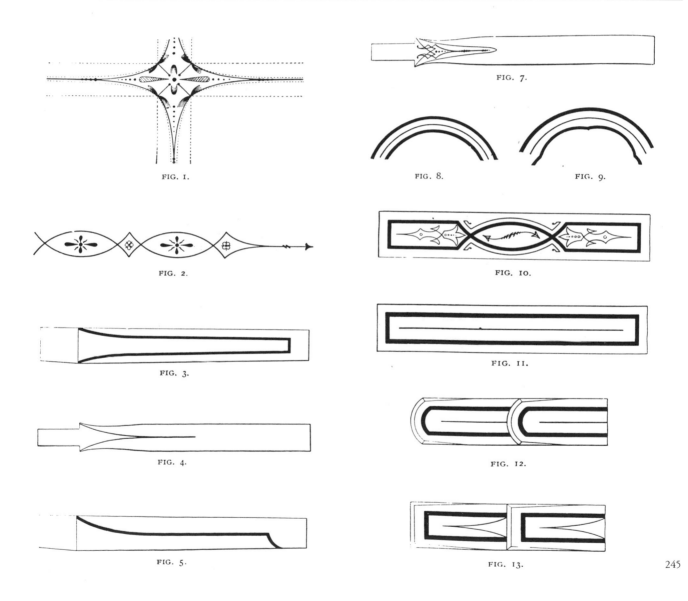

FIG. I.

FIG. 2.

FIG. 3.

FIG. 4.

FIG. 5.

FIG. 7.

FIG. 8.　FIG. 9.

FIG. 10.

FIG. II.

FIG. 12.

FIG. 13.

245

244. Panel designs. A selection of fine-line designs for panels and posts. The two designs at the top and the one at the bottom can be substituted for the one shown in the center of the panel, if the panel is long enough. *The Hub,* vol. 43, Feb. 1902. p. 497.

245. Wagon striping. Fig. 1: rib striping for a ribbed delivery body. Fig. 2: belt striping, where the width of a wagon is of a single board. Figs. 3–7: spoke striping. Figs. 8 & 9: rim striping. Figs. 10–13: spring striping. *The Hub,* vol. 37, Apr. 1895, p. 56.

246

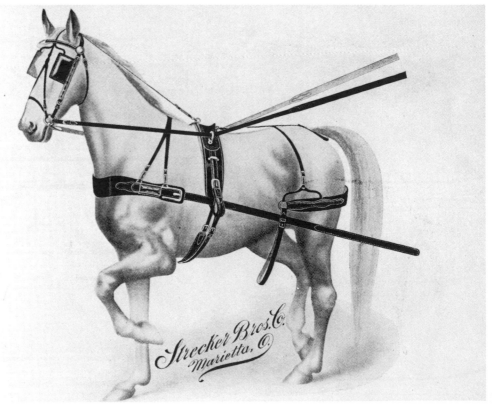

247

246. Single express harness. This common harness was used with delivery wagons, although many did not have spots (the small, round metal decorations) or kidney drops (the decorative pendants between the saddle and the breeching). Strecker Bros. Co., Marietta, Ohio, catalog, ca. 1921, p. 168.

247. Breast-collar delivery harness. Less common for commercial work than the round collar, this was often used for grocery delivery, R.F.D. mail wagons and other light-delivery types. Strecker Bros. Co., Marietta, Ohio, catalog, ca. 1921, p. 89.

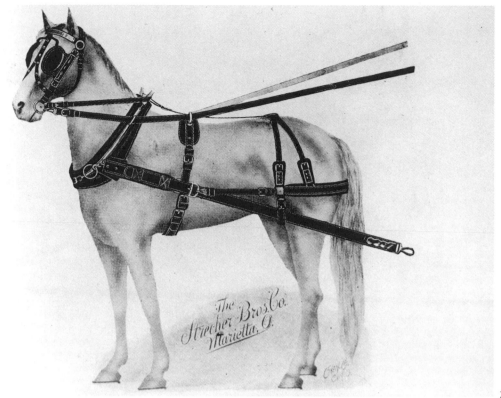

248

249

248. Single farm harness. One of the numerous styles of harness used with a one-horse farm wagon. Strecker Bros. Co., Marietta, Ohio, catalog, ca. 1921, p. 173.

249. Cart harness. Used with such vehicles as a two-wheel dray, dumpcart, etc., this harness has a broad saddle to distribute the part of the vehicle's weight that was borne by the horse. A support chain rested in the groove on top of the saddle, its ends attached to hooks on the shafts. Trace chains and hold-back chains were attached to a second and third hook on each shaft. Strecker Bros. Co., Marietta, Ohio, catalog, ca. 1921, p. 176.

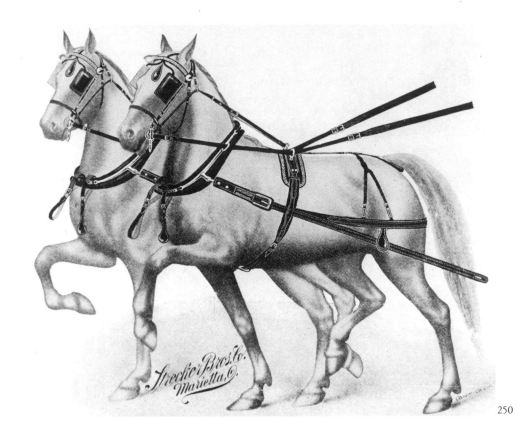

250

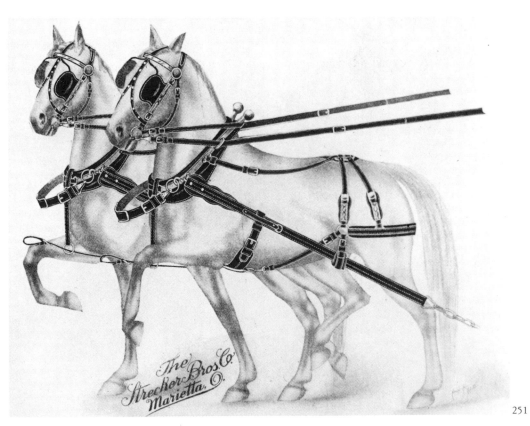

251

250. Hearse or hack harness. This double driving harness is of a type often used with some pleasure carriages. Strecker Bros. Co., Marietta, Ohio, catalog, ca. 1921, p. 218.

251. Truck harness. For use with trucks, drays and other heavy commercial vehicles. Strecker Bros. Co., Marietta, Ohio, catalog, ca. 1923, p. 284.

252

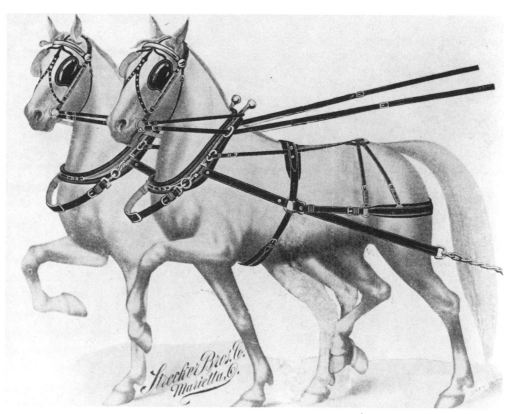

253

252. Truck harness. Similar to harness in no. 251, this was heavily decorated with spots and had a backband. Strecker Bros. Co., Marietta, Ohio, catalog, ca. 1921, p. 308.

253. Farm harness. This is similar to the single farm harness, but has breast straps (sometimes chains), which were attached in turn to the pole chains by which the horses steered, backed and held back the wagon. Strecker Bros. Co., Marietta, Ohio, catalog, ca. 1921, p. 316.

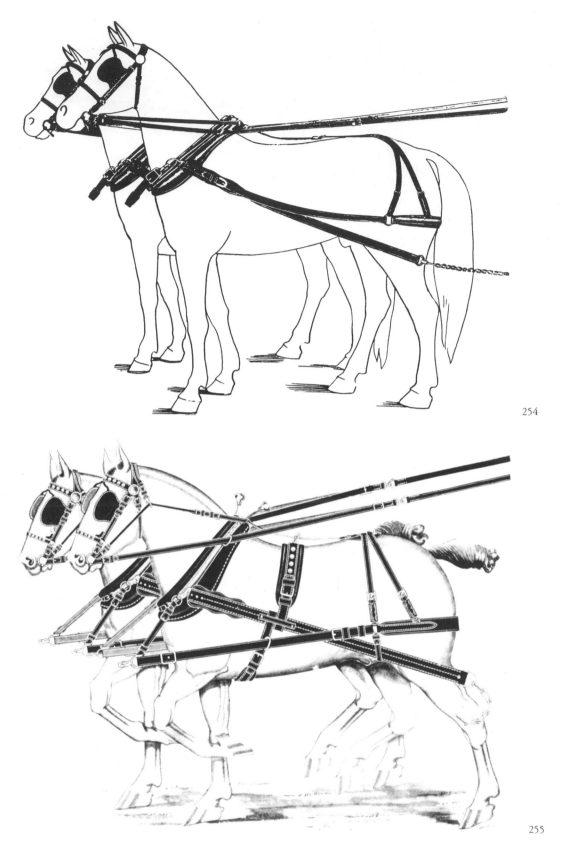

254

255

254. Double New York express harness. Here is a simplified harness, popular in New York City, that could be used with an express wagon or heavier delivery wagon. Smith, Worthington & Co., New York City, catalog, 1901, p. 102.

255. Double-team harness. This wagon harness varies from the type using breast chains or straps by employing side backers, straps through which steering and backing were accomplished. They extended from the breechings to the breast yokes. The Perkins-Campbell Co., New York City, catalog, 1925, p. 255.